NOIR CITY
OFFICIAL MAGAZINE OF THE FILM NOIR FOUNDATION

ANNUAL FIFTEEN

The Best of **NOIR CITY** Magazine

2022

PUBLISHED BY THE FILM NOIR FOUNDATION
San Francisco | Los Angeles | New York

NOIR CITY ANNUAL 15: The Best of NOIR CITY 2022

Copyright © 2023 by the Film Noir Foundation. All rights reserved. Printed in the United States of America. No part of this book may be used or reproduced in any manner whatsoever without written permission except in the case of brief quotations embedded in critical articles or reviews. For additional information, contact the Film Noir Foundation, 1411 Paru Street, Alameda, CA 94501 or visit filmnoirfoundation.org.

All proceeds from the sale of this book go directly to the non-profit Film Noir Foundation's mission to find and preserve *films noir* in danger of deterioration, damage or loss, and to ensure that high quality prints of these classic films remain in circulation for, we hope, theatrical exhibition to future generations.

Interested in contributing to *NOIR CITY Magazine*? Contact us at mailbox@filmnoirfoundation.org. Accepted submissions are published with the permission of the authors and the Film Noir Foundation claims no exclusive rights to the material.

FIRST EDITION

Cover and book design by Michael Kronenberg

ISBN 979-8-218-19985-2

FRONT COVER: *T-Men* (1947), Italian poster.
FRONTISPIECE: John Garfield and Lana Turner in *The Postman Always Rings Twice* (1946).
BACK COVER: *Double Indemnity* (1944), lobby card.

INTRODUCTION

IN PRAISE OF PLAN B

It was always my ambition to be a novelist. In my teens, I'd considered a career as a comic book illustrator and I left art school pondering life as a filmmaker. But I am, at heart, a writer. A wordsmith. And novels, to me, are the singular test of a writer's mettle. Singular—as in solitary. It's just you and blank pages, a void waiting for words that must coalesce into a story. I achieved my goal in 2002 with publication of *The Distance*, the first of what was to be a series of novels featuring a mid-20th-century sportswriter named Billy Nichols, a character based on my father. Although the book garnered excellent reviews and some genre-specific awards and nominations, Billy's time in the spotlight ended up being brief.

Prior to the publication of that debut novel, I'd been invited by the American Cinematheque in Hollywood to program and host a film festival based on my non-fiction book, *Dark City: The Lost World of Film Noir*. Looking back, I see this period, now almost 25 years ago, as the turning point in my life. *The Distance* won a "Shamus" Award from the Private Eye Writers of America for Best First Novel, while *Dark City: The Lost World of Film Noir* and a follow-up, *The Art of Noir*, would be nominated for Edgar Awards (from the Mystery Writers of America) as "Best Critical Non-Fiction." When I produced the inaugural NOIR CITY festival in San Francisco in 2003, my self-centered intention was to use the publicity to sell more novels. But just as NOIR CITY was taking off, the publisher, Scribner, pulled the plug on Billy. We didn't sell enough copies to merit continuation beyond a second installment (*Shadow Boxer*, 2003). I was informed of the cancellation at the annual Bouchercon mystery-lovers convention, where *The Distance* was nominated as Best First Novel.

You know the old adage: When one door closes, another opens. Frustration over losing my fiction deal soon became frustration over not being able to find good prints of lesser-known films for the increasingly popular NOIR CITY fests. That led me to create, in 2005, the Film Noir Foundation. At the time, I had about 100 pages written on a third Billy Nichols novel. Nineteen years later, I've completed about 175 pages. Billy may never emerge from limbo … because my fiction train got rerouted to another track — film festivals, restoration projects, a digital magazine, more non-fiction books, a publishing enterprise, and most visibly, a hosting (and writing) gig on Turner Classic Movies.

So, it was an especially pleasant surprise when the Mystery Writers of America chose me as a recipient of its cherished Raven Award, bestowed on someone for contributions to the genre "outside the realm of creative writing." Well, isn't *that* a neat plot twist. Wanting to follow in the tradition of novelists like Dashiell Hammett, Raymond Chandler, Leonard Gardner, and Paul Auster is what put me on this course, but more than twenty years later it's my work with the Film Noir Foundation (and TCM) that brought me this official and prestigious recognition.

I couldn't be more grateful. If the novels had been hits, who knows? I might have spent the last twenty-five years at home, writing scads of fiction in isolation. That would have been great (if it sold), but would it have been more fulfilling than being a film detective, resurrecting missing movies, acting as a lightning rod for passionate fans of the genre, and inspiring a new generation to appreciate "old movies?" *Hell, no.* All this may have begun as a fluke, but now it's a mission, one I'm thrilled to share with so many dedicated and talented colleagues in a collaborative, not a solitary, endeavor.

I may finish that third Billy Nichols book one of these days, but in the meantime … Plan B couldn't have worked out any better, mainly thanks to the loyal support and generosity of noir fans worldwide. Another wonderful aspect of Plan B becoming my *modus operandi* is that it has allowed me to work with, and help foster the careers, of so many other fabulous writers—as this anthology attests. Brilliant insights and fabulous writing await. Enjoy!

Darkly yours,
Eddie Muller

Odd Man Out (1947), directed by Carol Reed

NOIR CITY®

PUBLISHER
Eddie Muller

EDITOR-IN-CHIEF
Vince Keenan

MANAGING EDITOR
Steve Kronenberg

ART DIRECTOR/DESIGNER
Michael Kronenberg

**PROMOTIONAL DIRECTOR
EDITING/PRINT PRODUCTION**
Daryl Sparks

COPY EDITOR
Rachel Walther

NEWS EDITOR
Anne M. Hockens

EDITOR-AT-LARGE
Alan K. Rode

WEB MASTER
Ted Whipple

**FILM NOIR FOUNDATION
BOARD OF DIRECTORS**
Foster Hirsch
Andrea Kasin
Anita Monga
Eddie Muller, President
Alan K. Rode

ADVISORY COUNCIL
Gwen Deglise
Dana Delany
James Ellroy
Bruce Goldstein
Vince Keenan
John Kirk
Dennis Lehane
Leonard Maltin
Rose McGowan
Jon Mysel
Greg Olson
Fernando Martín Peña
Michael Schlesinger
Imogen Sara Smith
Todd Wiener

You've seen the movie... now read the book!

JAY DRATLER

Pitfall
Directed by André De Toth, starring Dick Powell & Elizabeth Scott (1948)

MARTY HOLLAND

Fallen Angel
Directed by Otto Preminger, starring Dana Andrews, Alice Faye & Linda Darnell (1945)

LOIS EBY & JOHN C. FLEMING

Larceny
Directed by George Sherman, starring John Payne, Joan Caulfield & Dan Duryea (1948)

EDNA SHERRY

Sudden Fear
Directed by David Miller, starring Joan Crawford, Jack Palance & Gloria Grahame (1952)

STARK HOUSE PRESS
1315 H Street, Eureka, CA 95501
707-498-3135 StarkHousePress.com

Available from your local bookstore or direct from the publisher.

ROBERT PRESTON

TABLE OF CONTENTS

ESSAYS

22 Down in the Depths
Román Viñoly Barreto and Argentinian Noir
By Imogen Sara Smith

36 Deadly Kisses, Scarlet Signals
On the Many Roles of Lipstick in Noir
By Nora Fiore

46 Unsafe Spaces
Paranoid Visions of Higher Education
By Jake Hinkson

56 The Big Rubdown
Masseurs and Masseuses in Film Noir
By Brent Calderwood

66 Merry X-Mas
The Small-Town Charms of *Cover Up*
By Bob Sassone

70 Horror Films: Noir Directors
By Sharon Knolle

82 Punk, Noir, and the Moon Upstairs
By Chris D.

PROFILES

94 Reluctant Hero
The Restless Charm of William Holden
By Rachel Walther

104 Stanley Baker
Loving a Thieving Boy
By Ray Banks

112 J.T. Walsh: Solid Cold
By Steve Kronenberg

122 Rolling the Bones for the Heavy Sugar
By John Wranovics

TABLE OF CONTENTS

132 **The Neo-Noir World of Claude Chabrol**
By Farran Smith Nehme

142 **Driving by Night with Paul Roberts**
By Jim Thomsen

148 **The Siren Song of Gale Sondergaard**
By Steve Kronenberg

158 **Veronica Lake**
Centenary
By Lynsey Ford

170 **Jim Nisbet**
Unleashed onto Life Itself
By Eddie Muller

INTERVIEWS

180 **John Dahl**
Modern Noir Master
By Sam Moore

194 **The Third Degree**
Melissa Errico
By Vince Keenan

APPRECIATIONS

200 **Prime Cuts: My Favorite Neo-Noir** *Carlito's Way*
By Danilo Castro

206 **Book vs. Film:** *Moonrise*
By Brian Light

212 **Book vs. Film:** *Out of the Past*
By Nora Fiore

"To find a modern pastiche of the noir/hardboiled novels of the 40s and 50s this good is quite rare."
— Booksplainer

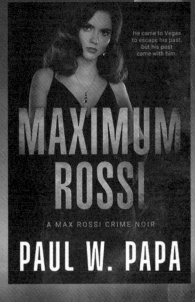
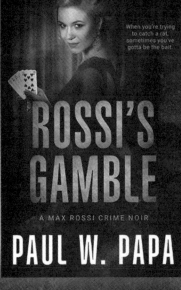
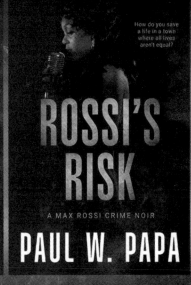

AVAILABLE ONLINE AND WHEREVER BOOKS ARE SOLD

ESSAYS
SECTION ONE

DOWN IN THE DEPTHS

Imogen Sara Smith

ROMÁN VIÑOLY BARRETO AND ARGENTINIAN NOIR

The Beast Must Die (1952) and The Black Vampire (1953) sound like a pair of horror movies, but there are no supernatural monsters here, only the many shades of human weakness, corruption, and cruelty. Elements of murder mystery, crime thriller, psychological melodrama, social criticism and, yes, terror, blend in these prime examples of Argentinian noir. Directed and co-written by Román Viñoly Barreto, *La bestia debe morir* (*The Beast Must Die*) and *El vampiro negro* (*The Black Vampire*) had never been officially released in the United States before their restoration, spearheaded by the Film Noir Foundation, and premieres at the NOIR CITY film festival. (*Beast* and *Vampire* are both available on disc from Flicker Alley.) Their return adds rich new territory to film noir's empire of shadows.

Born in 1910, Viñoly Barreto spent his early life in Uruguay, the first generation of his Spanish family to be born in South America. At nineteen he went to work for the national theater and was soon staging operas and plays, working with major European artists like conductor Arturo Toscanini and French actor Louis Jouvet on their visits to Montevideo. Uruguay was immensely wealthy at the time, a banking and communications center that, like neighboring Argentina, was spared the ruinous costs and destruction of World War II. In 1947, Viñoly Barreto was recruited to work in Argentina's booming film industry, which had its own studio system that, along with Mexico's, dominated cinemas throughout the Spanish-speaking world. Over the next twenty years, while continuing to work in the theater, his first love, Viñoly Barreto directed more than two dozen films in a variety of genres, including many comedies. His handful of noir films rank among his best and most personal. Daniel Viñoly, one of the director's sons, views many of his father's strongest films as "moral tales," grappling with issues of justice, vengeance, guilt, and reparation. A biblical scholar, Viñoly Barreto often appended quotations from scripture at the beginnings and ends of his films, yet the two I have seen are anything but moralizing. Instead, they harness his mastery of storytelling and visual style to lure you down treacherous paths, into some of the mind's darkest places.

The Human Beast

Based on a 1938 novel by Nicholas Blake, *The Beast Must Die* demonstrates Viñoly Barreto's skill at mingling genres, combining British detective story, lurid domestic soap opera, and noir-stained psychodrama. The opening plays like a parody of an Agatha Christie country-house whodunit, before flashbacks fill in the unspeakably painful loss at the root of the diabolical plot. There are layers of self-referentiality in this tale of a detective novel writer methodically planning a real homicide. The book's protagonist, Frank Carter, writes best-selling murder stories under the pseudonym Felix Lane, just as the

Ibáñez Menta with Romanian-born beauty Laura Hidalgo, who plays Linda.

Román Viñoly Barreto: stage and film director, translator, playwright, and biblical scholar.

Irish poet Cecil Day-Lewis (father of Daniel Day-Lewis) wrote them under the name Nicholas Blake. As Eddie Muller recounts in his liner essay to the film's Flicker Alley release, the book was inspired by an incident in which the author's son Sean was struck by a hit-and-run driver. It may seem ghoulish that he would proceed to imagine this non-fatal accident as a callous murder, with the small boy left to bleed to death in the road—but that's how writers are.

The novel was published in Argentina under the wonderfully named Seventh Circle imprint (akin to France's Série Noire), and Viñoly Barreto, a cultured and voracious reader whose tastes did not usually stoop to crime novels, loved its stark moral confrontation. The director added his own personal details to the film: a close-up of his hand stands in for the protagonist's when he writes in his journal, and the ill-fated son's well-loved, one-eyed teddy bear actually belonged to Viñoly Barreto's children. A slow pan around the son's room, taking in the stuffed bear and other toys, conveys with devastating simplicity the loss of an adored child. Such moments cut through the film's satire of melodramatic excess, which is underscored by slightly heightened, theatrical performances in the early scenes, and recurring shots of waves thunderously crashing on rocks. A vital clue is provided by a lonely provincial woman obsessed with movie stars, and when Felix Lane visits a film set to track down an actress, he finds her performing a wildly over-the-top gypsy dance number that caricatures movies as kitschy escapism.

Viñoly Barreto directing Ibáñez Menta.

Spanish-born actor Narciso Ibáñez Menta was best known for his roles in horror films.

These touches set up a dynamic tension between narrative or stylistic formulas, and the raw emotional and moral dilemmas that lie beneath.

The first detective story convention to be introduced is a murder victim hated by so many people that, when he drops dead at the dinner table, suspects abound. ("I'd better hurry up and kill him before someone else does," Felix muses at one point.) The aptly named Rattery (Guillermo Battaglia) is an arrogant, brutish patriarch who beats his meek wife, torments his sensitive stepson, and sees every attractive woman as fair game. Amid the handsome trappings of upper-class life, the film exposes a society poisoned by unchecked male power and a culture of toxic machismo. The elegantly layered script for *The Beast Must Die* is credited jointly to Viñoly Barreto and the film's star, Narciso Ibáñez Menta, who plays Frank/Felix. However, Daniel Viñoly told me that his father wrote all of his films more or less single-handedly, but had a "strange compulsion" to conceal the extent of his contributions, using pseudonyms or sharing credit with "anybody that would pop into his head." (Alberto Etchebehere, the cinematographer on *The Beast Must Die*, gets cowriting credit for *The Black Vampire*.)

Viñoly Barreto carefully planned out his films shot by shot in advance, and his closest working relationships were with cinematographers and editors. The attention to details of setting and costumes in *The Beast Must Die*, and the sly foregrounding of objects, are Hitchcockian: the Master himself could not do better at fusing the domestic and the sinister than a strangely ominous close-up of a sugar cube soaking up the darkness of coffee. The vehicular murder was filmed on a fog-flooded soundstage, giving it the claustrophobic feeling of a nightmare.

The ghastliness of this scene where the father finds his little boy—one tiny, bloodied hand grasping at the air—rips a hole in his psyche; he emerges after an unspecified time in a sanitarium with ashen hair and beard. Ibáñez Menta, a Spanish actor distinguished in theater, film, and television, revered Lon Chaney and shared his chameleonic range, but gives a beautifully stripped-down performance as a man hollowed out by grief. The movie's script sidelines the book's detective, Nigel Strangeways, to keep the focus on Felix Lane. As in the "black angel" plot beloved by Cornell Woolrich, Felix's righteous quest for vengeance turns him into a ruthless monomaniac, who uses the plotting skills honed on frivolous potboilers to coldly eliminate his son's killer. He doesn't hesitate to woo Rattery's sister-in-law, Linda (Laura Hidalgo), in order to gain access to the house, taking advantage of an emotionally fragile woman harassed by her brother-in-law's unwanted attentions. His scheme becomes messily entangled with real feelings, especially in a painful scene where he slaps Linda for drunkenly grabbing the teddy bear he has kept as a relic. A further complication arises in the form of Rattery's abused stepson, Ronnie (Humberto Balado), who attaches himself to Felix and sees him as a surrogate father. Ronnie reminds Felix of his own son, Martie, offering a fleeting promise of redemption for both. Like the confused little boy in Carol Reed's *The Fallen Idol* (1948), Ronnie tries to protect his hero, but his meddling only fouls up a perfect crime, leading to a mercilessly ironic final twist. Fate or accident, proper retribution or cruel irony? The ending leaves us with a sea of questions.

The Murderer Among Us

A man's eyes fill the screen in the opening moments of *The Black Vampire*, shadowy pools of confused pain. Smoke swirls, and the eyes dissolve into fragmentary visions: a woman laughing derisively; a frightened child; the cage of an elevator. Shown a series of Rorschach blots and asked to describe what he sees, the man murmurs feebly, "I don't know . . . I don't know . . . I don't know." This expressionistic montage plunges us once again into the mind of a killer, but raises a very different set of puzzles about guilt, responsibility, and punishment.

Coming to this movie cold, you might not immediately guess that it is based on Fritz Lang's *M* (1931), whose working title was "The Murderer Among Us." An innovative masterpiece of early sound cinema and one of the key ancestors of film noir, *M* was itself inspired by the real case of a serial killer known as the "Vampire of Dusseldorf." In Lang's coldly brilliant anatomy, the primal hor-

Like Fritz Lang's *M*, *The Black Vampire* draws a disturbing parallel between the innocence of childhood and a childlike killer tormented by his compulsions.

Olga Zubarry won the Silver Condor for Best Actress for her performance in *The Black Vampire*.

ror of a child-killer on the loose shears away the surface of society to uncover its callous and corrupt systems, revealing the law and the criminal underworld as ethically indistinguishable. The killer—played by a chubby, pop-eyed Peter Lorre in one of the most unsettling performances of all time—is a pitiful figure tortured by his compulsions. Joseph Losey's Hollywood remake, also titled *M* (1951), holds up astonishingly well, thanks to neorealist-style location shooting in the down-at-heel Bunker Hill neighborhood of Los Angeles, and a chillingly persuasive performance by the rodent-faced David Wayne. But both films relegate females to helpless and largely faceless victims; if Lang's *M* has one flaw, it is a moment of tacked-on finger-wagging that seems to blame neglectful mothers for the killing of their daughters. *The Black Vampire* is less a remake than a wholesale reimagining of *M*, and its most heartening change is to put a woman front and center.

She is Rita (Olga Zubarry), a singer in a seedy nightclub who is reluctantly drawn into a police investigation after catching a horrifying glimpse of a man dumping a child's body into a sewer. Rita is neither a saintly heroine nor a scapegoat, but a brave, sometimes blinkered working mother, just trying to keep her head down, raise her daughter, and hide the truth of her disreputable job. Like Linda in *The Beast Must Die*, she is embittered by a world in which men—even upright representatives of the law—treat her as a plaything. Her story is interwoven with that of Professor Teodoro Ulber (Nathán Pinzón), who leads a double life as a mousy professor of English, and as a goblin who stalks the streets looking for unaccompanied little girls. A shy misfit, he is tormented by women's mockery—this story bluntly illustrates Margaret Atwood's epigram: "Men's greatest fear is that women will laugh at them. Women's greatest fear is that men will kill them." Usually a comic actor (in *The Beast Must Die* he plays a nebbishy, cuckolded husband who salves his humiliation by shooting rats in his garage), here Pinzón uses his doughy, sad-clown face to instill a queasy mixture of pity and terror. He deliberately cuts his fingers with a broken glass, and peace settles over his face at the sight of blood. Even more disturbing is the way he clings

Like criminals in Carol Reed's *The Third Man* and Anthony Mann's *He Walked by Night*, the killer in *The Black Vampire* takes refuge in the sewers.

to children because they alone don't make fun of him: he weeps over a doll after murdering its owner, and on a roller coaster with another intended victim, he looks more terrified than the girl he clutches.

He is captured, in the end, not by underworld kingpins, as in Lang's *M*, but by "untouchables" who survive by scavenging in the sewers. (In one of the few touches imported directly from Lang's film, Ulber is recognized by a blind toy seller because he whistles Grieg's "In the Hall of the Mountain King.") The marginalized become defenders of the society that renders them outcasts—by ganging up on someone more beyond the pale than they are. Even the light seems tainted in *The Black Vampire*, lensed by Aníbal González Paz. Phantasmagoric visions bubble up, as if from under the surface of oily sewer water, and images struggle not to be swallowed by shadows and dragged down into the murk. Everyone moves through a grungy, constricted world of tunnels, alleys, smoky nightclubs, cage elevators, and cramped apartments. They are all trapped, one way or another.

In this world, the innocence of childhood is menaced not just by one sick man, but by a pervasive miasma of sordidness. The nightclub where Rita sings is filled with coarse, dissipated, leering faces. Her screams, upon seeing the killer through a window in her subterranean dressing room, filter up to the dance floor, where a woman casually remarks to her partner, "I also like to be beaten, but I don't scream." After Ulber kills a girl in an apartment block, a woman selfishly lies about a man found in the building, protecting her reputation while allowing her lover to be suspected. The film's ostensible hero, the investigative judge Dr. Bernard (Roberto Escalada), is frustrated in his marriage to a disabled woman and lusts after the vital, sexy Rita. But despite all the ugliness it depicts, *The Black Vampire* is ultimately a more empathetic film than *M*, and in some ways a scarier one, because its horror is not impersonal but directed at people we have come to care about. Once again, Viñoly Barreto made the film personal, this time by casting his daughter (credited only by her nickname, Gogó) as the central, beloved and endangered child.

The film's real climax is not the trial at the end, but a scene where Rita must face down the cornered, panicked killer and talk him into letting her daughter go. Armed police are massed around, but they are helpless to do anything but get the child killed. In this moment, everything depends not on men's guns, but on a woman's words.

A Nervous Country

When I asked Daniel Viñoly about how the European sources for these two films had been adapted to an Argentine setting, his answer was, essentially: not at all. They didn't need to be adapted, he quipped, because Argentinians of that era "thought they were Europeans." *The Beast Must Die* keeps the English character names and is largely set in a mock-Tudor mansion that could be in Sussex; in *The Black Vampire*, some street signs are in German, as if the setting were not Buenos Aires but Berlin. Unlike Mexico or the Andean countries, Argentina retained few traces of Indigenous culture—though Viñoly Barreto later directed several films about the overlooked plight of native peoples in the northern part of the country, projects that were deeply personal and important to him. Instead, Argentina's national culture was shaped by immigration from Italy, Spain, and Germany, and by an influx of Jewish intellectuals fleeing Nazi-occupied Europe. The country is famous for having more shrinks per capita than any other nation, and this devotion to psychotherapy has been attributed to the complexities of Argentinian identity.

Film noir flourished in Argentina during the postwar period when it swept the world, but the war itself, which cast such a long shadow in European, Japanese, and American films, played a minor role in Argentinian noir. The country had plenty of other things on its mind during the first two terms of President Juan Domingo Perón (1946–55), a controversial figure alternatively seen as a champion of the

The plot of *Hardly a Criminal* turns on a loophole in Argentine law that limits the sentence for embezzlement at six years—no matter how much you steal.

Fernando Ayala, director of *Los tallos amargos*, would in the 1960s become a reliable purveyor of more mainstream commercial movies.

working classes or a repressive demagogue who waged a bitter war against intellectuals and artists. Both before and after the military coup that overthrew Perón in 1955, the nation was riven by arguments over class, economic inequality, and national identity, generating the kind of instability and anxiety that form a fertile ground for noir.

Buenos Aires is introduced as "the nervous city" in *Hardly a Criminal* (*Apenas un delicuente*, 1949), a hard-edged story driven by twin engines of greed and betrayal. It was the last film made in Argentina by director Hugo Fregonese before he decamped for Hollywood—and Tinseltown did nothing to soften his edges, as evidenced by the gleefully brutal gem *Black Tuesday* (1954). *Hardly a Criminal* is steeped in caustic irony, following the shortcut-to-hell journey of a bank clerk who embezzles a fortune, intending to enjoy his loot after a short stint in jail; alas, his fellow inmates prove that when it comes to avarice and criminal cunning, he's only a piker. Actor Jorge Salcedo makes a charismatic antihero, with his handsome eyes and cool insolence, but his character is undone by his own cheap cynicism, easily rooked into suspecting his straight-arrow brother of stealing his bundle.

The look of *Hardly a Criminal* is all grit and daylight, with panoramas of seething crowds and roiling traffic in sunstruck city streets. At the other end of the visual spectrum is *Never Open That Door* (*No abras nunca esa puerta*, 1952), an omnibus film of two Cornell Woolrich short stories[1]. Director Carlos Hugo Christensen and cinematographer Pablo Tabernero lavish the film with velvety, soot-black shadows, gleaming backlighting, sinuous camera moves, and complex deep-focus shots. By far the stronger of the two sections is the second, "Hummingbird Comes Home," one of the few truly

---

1 A third tale, entitled *Si muero antes de despertar* (*If I Should Die Before I Wake*) was released separately as a 73-minute feature. The film has been preserved by the Film Noir Foundation, which hopes to do a digital restoration.

successful cinematic representations of blindness. The aging woman at the center of the story starts out literally and figuratively blind: she rejoices at the return of her long-absent son before the shattering realization that he has become a thuggish criminal who is on the run with his equally unsavory associate. In a long, silent sequence, the mother (Ilde Pirovano) moves through her home at night, pocketing the men's guns, locking them in their rooms, and cutting the lights. "Now we're all equal," she declares grimly, "Everybody blind." The suspense of this daringly minimalist sequence builds to a sensational climax when the woman, her face completely erased by darkness, pulls a gun from her apron and points it at the sound of someone coming down the stairs, not knowing if she is about to shoot her only son.

The ironic twists keep coming in Fernando Ayala's *The Bitter Stems* (*Los tallos amargos*, 1956), another masterpiece restored by the Film Noir Foundation and released by Flicker Alley. The clever, unpredictable story, based on an award-winning novel by Adolfo Jasca, revolves around a relationship between two men: the neurotically insecure Gasper (Carlos Cores), a journalist with a stalled career, and the charming, shady Liudas (Vassili Lambrinos), an undocumented Hungarian immigrant addicted to get-rich-quick schemes. For once, it is neither money nor sex that tempts the protagonist; it is a thwarted dream of heroism, of serving some great cause. (A lushly Freudian, symbol-laden dream sequence does the work of a more conventional expository flashback—or a session on a psychiatrist's couch.) Gasper is a born follower, easily seduced by Liudas's plans for a fake correspondence school that will earn money to save his family from political turmoil in Europe. But insecurity curdles into paranoia when Gasper suspects his friend of playing him for a sucker, and his seeming ineffectuality gives way to chillingly sociopathic violence. The whole story turns on miscues, misunderstandings, and revelations that come too late.

The sublime cinematography by Chilean-born Ricardo Younis combines the jagged expressionist shadows of a Weimar-era German horror movie with the sultry atmosphere of a tropical night, heavy and charged with a coming thunderstorm. The musical score by Astor Piazzolla, who revolutionized the tango, perfectly matches the film's blend of torrid emotion and cerebral sharpness. The characters, cast, and creators all represent the multicultural tapestry of Argentina's immigrant society. The rescue of a film like this, or the two by Viñoly Barreto, all of which came perilously close to being lost and forgotten, should remind us that film history has all too often been distorted by the absence or availability of prints. Each discovery makes the bitter little world a bit larger. ∎

The author thanks Daniel Viñoly for his generous assistance.

Carlos Cores in *The Bitter Stems*, which was included in *American Cinematographer*'s list of the 100 best-photographed films of all time.

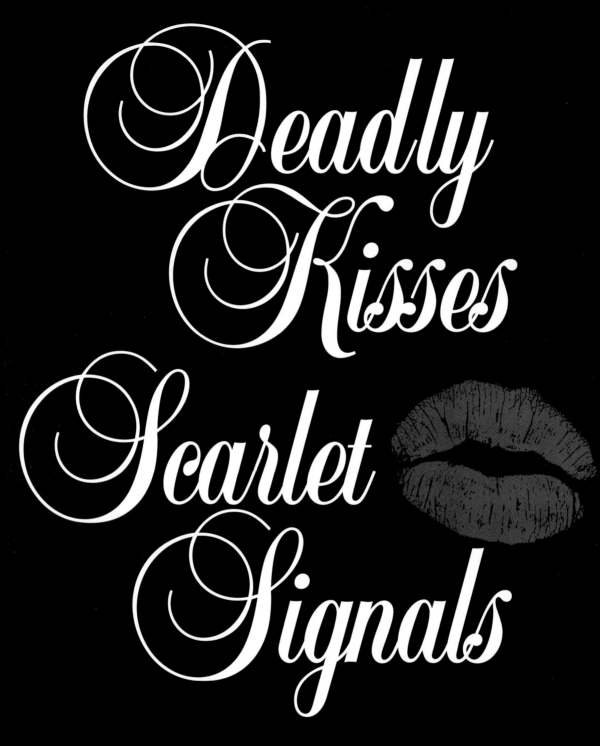

Deadly Kisses Scarlet Signals

ON THE MANY ROLES OF LIPSTICK IN NOIR

Nora Fiore

mbushed in the opulence of her Mexico City hotel suite, Jane Palmer (Lizbeth Scott) is cornered. And dangerous. Avenging killjoy Don Blake (Don DeFore) watches Jane's every move as she reaches for her purse.

"Looking for something?" Don asks.
"My lipstick," she lies.
"Colt or Smith & Wesson?"

It's one of *Too Late for Tears*' best wisecracks, the juxtaposition of lipstick and guns evoking a femme fatale's versatile threat. She can destroy men using beauty, bullets—or both. The lethal ladies of film noir would likely agree that lipstick is "a woman's weapon in a man's world," as *Glamour* magazine asserted in 1941.

The ubiquity of that "woman's weapon" in classic movies, noir or otherwise, is hardly surprising. Hollywood sold glamour, and glamour sold Hollywood. Fan magazines and exhibitors' trade journals of the era abound with tie-ins between cosmetics and films, retailers, and movie theaters. For example, women in 1944 might have bought a ticket for *Double Indemnity* after seeing an ad at the Max Factor counter of their local department store.

Noir explored the rich emotional and narrative potential of lipstick on film. Wielded by designing women, this everyday item illustrates the paradox of being seen without being passive. Applying lipstick in *The Postman Always Rings Twice*, Lana Turner entices the spectator to gaze upon her beauty while highlighting the vanity and calculation behind it. From *Phantom Lady*'s righteous Carol to *Leave Her to Heaven*'s despicable Ellen, noir women across the moral spectrum deploy lipstick as a tool, literally painting themselves as they wish to be seen. Filmmakers, writers, and actors used the language of lipstick to communicate with audiences in myriad ways, create dramatic tension, and even smuggle risqué subtext past the censors.

Lipstick as Wartime Glamour
THIS GUN FOR HIRE (1942)

Some women would squawk at finding their last five bucks stolen. Not seasoned trouper Ellen Graham (Veronica Lake). In the gloom of an overnight chair car, she roots around her satchel for a lipstick. (Don't ask *why* she's looking for her lipstick in the middle of the night on a train. Screen goddesses are unbound by such logic.) Ellen discovers the theft, but doesn't sound the alarm. Instead, she pulls out the lipstick and huskily confronts the contract killer in the next seat as she touches up her makeup.

Nothing builds up a glamour girl in the public eye like loving close-ups, and the luscious nighttime series on the train delivers for Lake. In John F. Seitz's lighting, her freshly painted mouth offsets her pale, delicate features and the shimmering curves of her hair. As the actress wrote in her autobiography, *This Gun for Hire* "certainly helped perpetuate Veronica Lake as Everyman's mistress."

Ellen's on-the-go glamour aligns with World War II–era notions of femininity as a form of resilience and winning morale. "If a symbol were needed of this fine, independent spirit—of this courage and strength—I would pick a lipstick," proclaimed Tangee company head Constance Luft Huhn (or some canny copywriter) in a 1943 ad. Resourceful singer-illusionist-spy Ellen embodies that "courage and strength" by facing down a tough character while freshening her lipstick.

Lipstick as Disguise
PHANTOM LADY (1944)

In Cornell Woolrich's novel, the heroine's wild night of jazz, deception, and peril begins in the privacy of her apartment. Before a mirror, she appraises her disguise, a "catalogue of sleazy accessibility," then invokes her lover with a "little prayer" of hope. By contrast, director Robert Siodmak introduces the transformed Carol Richman (Ella Raines) with a visual wolf whistle. Tilting upward, the camera seems to drool over her hep kitten disguise, from the ankle-strap heels to the dolled-up face, complete with a beauty mark and broadly drawn lips.

The film's Carol processes her feelings of degradation before a mirror, not in the security of her apartment but rather in the eye of a musical storm. Sickened by the forceful smooch of drummer Cliff (Elisha Cook Jr.) in an underground jive joint, "Jeannie" sidles over to a grimy mirror. With assured strokes, she reapplies her lipstick. But then the whole of the face—a face both hers and not hers—seems to hit Carol. She shakes herself and stares at the strange woman staring back. Raines invests the moment with a shiver of uncanny self-discovery. We can almost hear Carol thinking, *"Is that me?"*

The jazz sequence fragments Carol's body: legs by the drums, torso by the piano, grinning head by the trumpet. Holding her lipstick, the intrepid sleuth has to pull herself together. In that oneiric vortex of rhythm, booze, drugs, and desire, the virtuous sleuth glimpses the dark side of determination. She realizes that the boundaries of her identity might not hold up against her disguise and her desperation for the truth. How far outside of herself will she go to save her man?

Lipstick as Innuendo
DOUBLE INDEMNITY (1944)

"Hope I've got my face on straight." Phyllis Dietrichson (Barbara Stanwyck), now fully covered, glides toward the camera then turns to primp at the mirror. While Walter Neff (Fred MacMurray) hovers behind her, his leering grin in the reflection, Phyllis draws a lipstick along her mouth with a no-nonsense scrubbing motion. This intimate ritual, part of redressing after her sunbath, is just one move in Phyllis's erotic performance for Neff that fateful afternoon. Lipstick is a key component of the devious housewife's appeal. The garish, overdrawn shape of her mouth—"like a gash across her face," in the words of film historian Drew Casper—contributes to her overall impression of seductive cheapness.

Later, Phyllis's lipstick suggests the adulterous consummation that made *Double Indemnity* such a challenging property to adapt under the Motion Picture Production Code. Stanwyck had plenty of experience implying through reapplying, even during the pre-Code era. As office maneater Lily Powers in *Baby Face* (1933), Stanwyck coolly circles her mouth with lipstick after getting caught in flagrant delicto with a colleague. The lipstick cue operates similarly in Billy Wilder's noir.

After Phyllis appears at Walter's apartment, they drink their bourbon and settle on the sofa. Dis-

solves transport us to Walter's office, where his Dictaphone confession continues, then back to the dim, sterile apartment. The schemers remain fully clothed on the sofa. However, Walter's splayed relaxation and Phyllis's matter-of-fact application of lipstick are more than enough to hint at events that transpired during the ellipsis. Censors were no match for what Stanwyck could do with a lipstick.

Lipstick as Malice Aforethought
LEAVE HER TO HEAVEN (1945)

She wants to look as beautiful as possible when they find her at the bottom of the stairs; Ellen Berent (Gene Tierney) is dead set on that. So she plans one of the most aesthetically pleasing crimes in cinema. Ellen carefully costumes and stages her fall to kill "the little beast" inside of her. She selects the ice-blue peignoir and matching silk mules. In a mirror shot cluttered with chintz roses, ruffles, and suffocating, rancid prettiness, Ellen intently draws a lipstick around the curves of her already scarlet mouth.

Lipstick is more intrusively present throughout Technicolor thriller *Leave Her to Heaven* than it could be in any black-and-white noir. The viewer's eye wants to linger on the lush berry red of Tierney's bow lips, on the color applied so perfectly that it might have been tattooed on. Those lips enhance the unsettling impact of her teal eyes—especially when she gazes down the stairs in diabolical exultation.

Lipstick as Entrance and Exit
THE POSTMAN ALWAYS RINGS TWICE (1946)

No classic femme fatale is more defined by lipstick than diner siren Cora Smith (Lana Turner). Her lipstick precedes her. The white tube rolls across the floor with a hard rattle. The camera's gaze moves in the opposite direction, toward the open-toed heels and shapely gams in the doorway.

Cora's lipstick sparks a teasing battle of wills. She holds out her hand for the tube, but John Garfield's Frank Chambers leans insolently against the counter. With a sultry close-up, she comes to him, then turns her attention back to herself. Cora applies her lipstick as a coy parting shot, "preening . . . merely to show him plenty of what he can't have," as Jeanine Basinger describes. This opening exchange foreshadows the love-hate power struggle that fuels Cora and Frank's passion.

Turner's star entrance typifies the uneasy marriage between MGM's house style and James M. Cain's lean, grubby material. The novel's Cora makes a more mundane first appearance; she walks in from the kitchen to pick up Frank's dishes. The drifter zeroes in on one feature: "Her lips stuck out in a way that made me want to mash them in for her." Perhaps that line—and the kinky lip biting a few pages later—inspired the film's lipstick motif.

While rebuffing Frank's advances, Cora uses her lipstick to cut his ego down to size. Extricating herself from his rough embrace, she wipes her lips with a handkerchief, pulls out her white mirror, and redraws her scarlet pout. Cora's silent scorn and disgusted mouth movements tell Frank that he's a waste of makeup to her.

Lipstick bookends the film's portrayal of Cora. It announces her presence in the beginning, and it drops from her limp hand to represent her offscreen death. Returning from the beach, Cora cozies up with Frank in the front seat and applies lipstick with a kittenish joy previously lacking in her demeanor. She promises Frank "kisses with dreams in them," but their last kiss costs both of their lives. All of Cora's vain dreams and desires are reduced to that little white tube falling from her lifeless, long-nailed fingers.

Lipstick as Clue
DEADLINE AT DAWN (1946)

By the off-kilter glow of a lamp with a crooked shade, taxi dancer June Goffe (Susan Hayward) surveys the detritus of cryptic clues in the dead woman's room: cigarettes, lipstick, matchbook, white carnation. "This isn't her lipstick," June deduces, turning to look at the brunette lying on the floor. "It belongs to a blonde. Light." That logical leap may raise a few eyebrows. However, lipstick ads of the era, including Max Factor's, touted particular shades for blondes versus brunettes, brownettes, and redheads. Realistic or not, June's inference alludes to a system of feminine signifiers that a man might miss in the same situation. A woman sleuth reads the world differently.

After June correctly infers that a blonde is mixed up in the murder, she follows the mystery woman's trail from a soda fountain to a taxi to an apartment house. June eavesdrops on a bickering couple whose resentment simmers like the miserably hot night. Lipstick has pointed the way to the motive for murder: an unhappy wife and a marriage collapsing under the weight of infidelity.

Lipstick as Bribe and Metamorphosis
CAGED (1950)

The ladies of Corridor B eagerly daub their lips with the "Jungle Red" contraband. "I sure feel like a new woman," exclaims Helen (Sheila MacRae). Such is the transformative power of lipstick. The long-lasting commodity provides an instant psychological uplift for women stripped of their individuality by the prison system. Big-time racketeer Elvira Powell (Lee Patrick) could scarcely have chosen a better Christmas present to cement her status as the new queen bee of the cell block.

Vicious, venal guard Evelyn Harper (Hope Emerson) knows the value of beauty products; her black-market-in-a-drawer contains a stock of lipstick, along with powder and perfume. By supplying lipstick to the prisoners, Harper hopes to boost Elvira's popularity, then force Agnes Moorehead's Warden Benton to seize the precious gifts. As Benton walks past the inmates at the party, their glee dies away. Emma (Ellen Corby) wipes her mouth. Smoochie (Jan Sterling) holds out her tube for confiscation. However, the warden outsmarts Harper. She lets the prisoners keep their prize. In a cruel world, sometimes kindness is the shrewdest policy.

Lipstick signals the heroine's choice of freedom over the straight and narrow. Marie Allen (Eleanor Parker) snatches the rhinestone-studded compact she once rejected and applies lipstick in long, aggressive streaks. Thus Marie wordlessly agrees to Elvira's bargain. But what exactly are the terms? On the page, she'll join Elvira's syndicate in exchange for a fast parole. Between the lines, she may be sweetening the deal by becoming Elvira's moll. Parker turns the simple act of applying lipstick into a manifesto of defiant survival. Instead of conceding defeat, she takes control. No longer the scared teenager who entered prison, Marie swaps her shattered naiveté for the cynical confidence of a femme fatale. The lipstick cinches it: she has emerged a new woman.

Lipstick as Pathos
NIAGARA (1953)

The deed is done. George Loomis (Joseph Cotten) finally killed his bombshell wife. Attempting to flee the scene of the crime, he stumbles on the contents of his victim's purse, dumped in her frantic last minutes. Something glints on the floor, and he bends to pick it up. A close shot of the object radiates sensuality: a bright red lipstick in a gold tube, encrusted with multicolored rhinestones.

The lipstick epitomizes the hyperfeminine allure of Rose Loomis (Marilyn Monroe), but the context renders this glitzy object perverse and macabre. It is a dead woman's lipstick, held in the fingers of the man who murdered her. The image stings with regret and melancholy, a small, devastating detail in a film of crashing elemental forces.

Lipstick as Defense Mechanism
THE BIG HEAT (1953) AND *HUMAN DESIRE* (1954)

In two different Fritz Lang films, Gloria Grahame's doomed characters reach for lipstick when navigating precarious situations. As sadistic hood Vince Stone (Lee Marvin) begins grilling Debby Marsh about her evening's activities in *The Big Heat*, she pointedly avoids eye contact. Pausing at the marble mantle of Stone's apartment, Debby takes out her lipstick and leans into the mirror. The subject of Dave Bannion (Glenn Ford) comes up.

"He's got a hot flash for you," Debby says around the lipstick. She holds her mouth fixed and open for precise application, giving her face a taut, attractive vulgarity. The fixed lips, held firm for accuracy, force her tongue to do more work on the next sentence: "He hates your guts." What the words lack in enunciation, they make up for with an extra froth of spit and emphatic loathing. Smearing the bullet of color around her lips, Debby continues to stall.

The mirror close-ups of Grahame offer the viewer a last chance to appreciate Debby in all her splendor. "That's a real pretty kisser," Vince can't resist commenting with a threatening caress, moments before reaching for the hot coffee.

In *Human Desire*, Vicki—still reeling from her forced participation in a murder—must distract the man who could identify her husband. Once again forced to exploit her wiles and sex appeal to save her brutal spouse, she walks uncertainly through the train's shadowy corridor. She opens a compact and freshens her lipstick, blending with her little finger. The lipstick serves as a centering ritual. She steels herself and puts on a brave face for the next maneuver.

Lipstick as Modus Operandi
WHILE THE CITY SLEEPS (1956)

The camera looks up from the murdered woman's robe, crumpled on the floor and conjuring unhealthy images of offscreen savagery. A crime scene photographer steps away to reveal the lipstick scrawl on the wall: "Ask mother." This MO deliberately echoes the real-life 1945 murder of Frances Brown. Using the victim's lipstick, serial killer William Heirens wrote on her bathroom mirror: "For heavens Sake catch me Before I kill more I cannot control myself."

Just as the bloodthirsty Chicago press dubbed Heirens the "Lipstick Killer," dying media tycoon Amos Kyne (Robert Warwick) bestows the same gruesome sobriquet on his cinematic counterpart.

"How many women in the United States use lipstick?" the mogul asks. "How many women are there?" newspaper editor Jon Day Griffith (Thomas Mitchell) replies ironically.

"I want every one of them scared silly every time she puts any on," Kyne enthuses.

The hypocritical newshound sniffs out the powerhouse sensationalism of lipstick crossed with crime. Imagining their own lipsticks in the hands of a killer, millions of women can both relate to and shudder at this lurid detail.

More than headline bait, the lipstick message sheds light on the killer's psychological profile. As Ed Mobley (Dana Andrews) declares over the airwaves, "You're a mama's boy. . . . The normal feeling of love that you should have toward your mother has been twisted into hatred, for her and for all of her sex." Mobley hits the mark; Robert Manners (John Drew Barrymore) does blame his adopted parent for, he claims, wanting a girl, then grooming him as one. "Ask mother" both accuses his maternal figure and defers to her authority. Through murder, Robert violently rejects the femininity he felt his mother imposed on him. However, by picking up a feminine-coded possession of the victim's, he chooses a "woman's weapon" to send his message. ∎

For a full bibliography, visit: bit.ly/lipstickNC

MAR 10 1944

Barbara Stanwyck

SOON TO BE SEEN IN PARAMOUNT'S "DOUBLE INDEMNITY"

Tru-Color Lipstick

...the color stays on through every lipstick test

GLAMOROUS REDS, lovely reds, dramatic reds...all exclusive with Tru-Color Lipstick and all based on an original patented color principle discovered by *Max Factor Hollywood*...$1.00

ORIGINAL COLOR HARMONY SHADES FOR EVERY TYPE

BLONDE   BRUNETTE   BROWNETTE   REDHEAD

Complete your make-up IN COLOR HARMONY...WITH MAX FACTOR HOLLYWOOD FACE POWDER AND ROUGE

Max Factor - Hollywood

Unsafe Spaces

PARANOID VISIONS OF HIGHER EDUCATION

By Jake Hinkson

Welcome to Noir University! Although we associate film noir with police stations and smoky barrooms, it's interesting to note how many noirs made during the classic era were set in a more unlikely locale: the college campus. Far from viewing universities as places of knowledge and self-improvement, these films uncovered a menacing darkness beneath academia's genteel facade and, in the process, revealed a decidedly anti-intellectual strain of paranoia, one that has only grown over the years.

So strap in for a quick campus tour of Dark City's most dangerous institution of higher learning. The student body is made up of psychos, the teachers are creeps, and the tests can be murder—but, hey, at least you can smoke and drink in class.

FROM "GI JOE" TO "JOE COLLEGE"

One of the signature benefits of the Servicemen's Readjustment Act of 1944 (aka the GI Bill) was a dramatic increase in federal funding for higher education. With the help of the GI Bill, nearly eight million veterans (nearly *half* of the sixteen million who had served in the war) either pursued vocational training or went to college.

That didn't mean it was easy. The key word in the original bill's title, after all, was "readjustment," and that readjustment wasn't always a smooth process. There's a whole subgenre of noir about shellshocked soldiers getting out of the military psych ward only to find that the America they've returned to is a new and confusing place, and a few films even set that tortured readjustment on a college campus. Phil Karlson's *5 Against the House* (1955) follows a couple of Korean War vets (smooth Guy Madison and PTSD-plagued Brian Keith) trying to make a go of it studying law at Midwestern University. Along with a couple of buddies, they decide to rob a casino in Reno as a lark, or as one of them describes it, as a "field experiment in psychology." Things, as you might expect, do not go as planned.

5 Against the House is not a great film, despite having action maestro Karlson (*99 River Street* [1953]) at the helm and William Bowers (*Cry Danger*

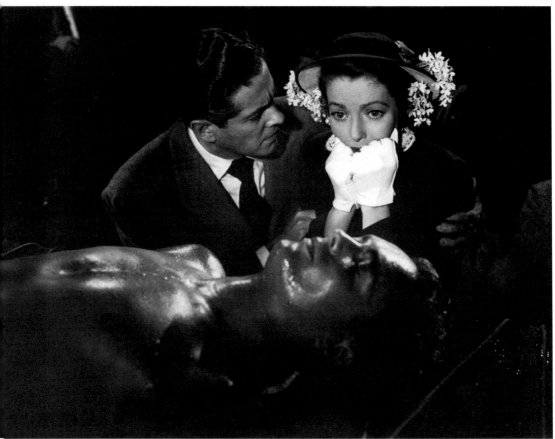

Warren Ford (Robert Cummings) helps Professor Wilma Tuttle (Loretta Young) confront the death of her student Bill Perry (Douglas Dick) in *The Accused*.

[1951]) among the screenwriters providing quips for the guys. While the film is plodding and uneven, it does nicely capture an unease with the whole college experience. One of the guys, robbery mastermind Ronnie (Kerwin Mathews), describes his state of mind as: "Bored. Bored with classes that have just begun and with notes I haven't taken yet. Bored with being in a place run by thinkers and not doers."

That line underscores a constant critique found in noir films exploring the academic life, namely that college is a place that mistakenly prioritizes thought over action. The central ambiguity at the heart of these films, however, is that the trouble always begins when the characters attempt to break free of academic life and explore the real world. The result is a conflicted message: to be a thinker is to be repressed and boring, but to try to break free and be a doer always ends in disaster.

We find an even darker ex-GI turned college student in *The Accused* (1949). Bill Perry (Douglas Dick) is fixated on his psychology professor,[1] Dr. Wilma Tuttle (Loretta Young). He is, in the parlance of the time, "fresh" with her, which today means that he has no boundaries. His backstory is left rather vague, but his guardian, Warren Ford (Robert Cummings), explains that Perry is "confused" and trying to "make up" for the years that he lost in the army during the war.

Perry is a great deal worse than confused, though; he is dangerous. When he tries to rape Dr.

---

1   The top academic field at Noir University is psychology. If you find a professor in a film noir, that person probably teaches psychology, usually with an emphasis on abnormal or criminal pathologies. The second-place field of study is law. There is no third place because aside from psychology and law, there appear to be no other courses taught at NU.

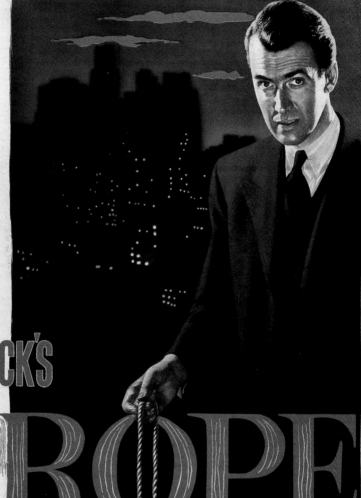

Worst dinner party ever? Homicidal schoolboys John Dall and Farley Granger (far right) test the theories of their mentor James Stewart (far left) in *Rope*.

Tuttle one night, she kills him and dumps his body in the ocean, trying to make his death look like an accident. The film, with a script by Ketti Frings (*The File on Thelma Jordon* [1949]) from the 1947 novel by June Truesdell, places a lot of emphasis on Dr. Tuttle's position as a woman in the world of academia. It's not just her lecherous student who keeps brushing aside her job title to remind her that she's a woman first and foremost, though. So does every other man in the film. One witness in the murder investigation tells her, "You're a professor? Maybe I should have gone more to school." The ostensibly sympathetic Ford compliments a dress she's wearing by telling her, "Your brains don't show a bit." All of this starkly dramatizes the sexism faced by professional women, even in the supposedly enlightened world of higher education (which is, in fact, one of the world's oldest boys' clubs). It also presents a sexist twist on the timeworn idea that education is just something repressed people use to try and escape "real" life—in this case, every man from her attempted rapist to the investigating police officer warns Dr. Tuttle that she's using her education to repress her femininity.

THE BOYS WHO STUDY TOO MUCH

Some films go beyond the fear of college as an institution that stifles real-life experience. In these films, we find a paranoia that education itself might be inherently bad, maybe even immoral. Intentional or not, these films portray a deep-seated mistrust of intellectuals, reveling in the suspicion that a brilliant mind is almost always a sick mind. Although there are many differences between Bill Perry in *The Accused* and the killers in *Rope* (1948) and *Compulsion* (1959), these nutjobs all have one thing in common: they're excellent students.

The obvious inspiration for both *Rope* and *Compulsion* was the case of Nathan Leopold and Richard Loeb, two students at the University of Chicago who murdered a fourteen-year-old boy

Dean Stockwell and Bradford Dillman as Leopold and Loeb (renamed Steiner and Straus) in *Compulsion*

named Bobby Franks in 1924. The resulting trial of Leopold and Loeb became a media sensation, and the narrative that emerged about them would influence a certain strain of crime film for decades to come. Intellectually gifted overachievers,[2] the killers were particularly obsessed with Nietzsche's idea of the *Übermensch*, that truly exceptional individual whose superior intellect lifts him above the morality necessary to constrain lesser men. The killers, the public was horrified to learn, essentially considered the murder of Bobby Franks a test of this intellectual premise.

In *Rope*, Leopold and Loeb are Brandon and Phillip (John Dall and Farley Granger), two Harvard students who strangle a classmate in their penthouse apartment, then stuff his body in a trunk and proceed to host a ghoulish dinner party around the hidden corpse. The unsuspecting guests at the party include the killers' former prep-school housemaster, Rupert Cadell (James Stewart), who gradually figures out what has happened. Dall and Granger are terrific as the killers, with Dall swaggering and superior, convinced of his own brilliance, while Granger spends the entire film in an emotional spiral, unable to contain his horror at what he has done.

Aside from the killers, the most contemptable character in the film is their bookish mentor, Cadell. A wicked vision of self-deluded intellectualism, he is a man who mesmerizes young boys with jokes about eugenics and murder, then flinches when they grow up and put his ideas to the test. In the final moments of the film, Cadell is given a long, self-absolving speech that is, to use a highbrow academic term, pure bullshit. Despite his self-righteous platitudes at the end, Stewart makes Cadell a coldly intellectual, slightly sinister presence. Which is, after all, the point. If *Rope* has a theme, that theme is that too much education makes people amoral monsters.

Based on the 1956 novel by Meyer Levin, a real-life classmate of Leopold and Loeb, Richard Fleischer's *Compulsion* hews much closer to the official record. The film makes no real effort to dis-

---

2   Leopold spoke five languages, and Loeb skipped so many grades he graduated from college at the age of seventeen.

Joan Bennett helps Professor Edward G. Robinson explore some psychological aspects of homicide in *The Woman in the Window*.

guise the fact that the young killers—renamed Steiner and Straus here—were lovers, and it explores the psychosis of their relationship vividly. Steiner is played with an icy fragility by Dean Stockwell. He's brilliant, knows seventeen languages, and can already outdebate his professors on Nietzsche, but he's also helplessly in love with Straus, portrayed by Bradford Dillman as a coddled, coldhearted psycho. Steiner might have the intellectual concepts, but Straus has the real ice in his veins. Drunk on a mix of narcissism and philosophical delusion, the two of them become one giant id. *Compulsion* dramatizes fairly explicitly (at least for a film of 1959) the paranoia that moral degeneration and sexual perversion go hand in hand with excessive education.

One final bookish murderer we should make note of has no obvious connection to Leopold and Loeb, though he would certainly fit in with their Nietzsche study group.[3] This is Larry Crain (Peter Cookson), antihero of director Alfred Zeisler's fascinating *Fear* (1946). Made at lowly Monogram, the story is a loose reworking of Dostoevsky's *Crime and Punishment*. In the novel, the murderer Raskolnikov is an ex-student who murders a pawn broker, but *Fear* shifts the narrative into the world of the university, where Crain, a penniless student about to be kicked out of school after funding for his scholarship dries up, decides to rob and kill his professor Dr. Stanley (Francis Pierlot), a usurious old man with a sideline loaning money to his cash-strapped students. Suspicion falls on Crain for the murder in part because of a journal article he writes entitled "Men Above the Law" that, in essence, argues the same pseudo-*Übermensch* philosophy that mesmerized Leopold and Loeb.[4] Although *Fear* is a low-rent affair, with an unfortunate tacked-on happy ending, the picture it paints of university

---

3   Nietzsche is Noir U's most commonly cited philosopher. There is no runner-up.
4   Although the movie ignores most of *Crime and Punishment*, this plot point is taken directly from the novel, where Raskolnikov publishes a similar article, titled "On Crime." This is where you find Nietzsche and Dostoevsky colliding, at least in the world of Poverty Row film noir. What those writers have in common with the films discussed here comes down to a preoccupation with one fundamental question: If God doesn't exist, then isn't everything permissible?

Lydia (Mary McLeod) comforts her stressed-out quasi-boyfriend, Paul Cartwright (Jimmy Lydon), at the end of *Strange Illusion*.

life is among the bleakest of the period. In this film, college is a place where the professors are miserly grifters who take all your money then leave you to subsist on cold soup and a morally bankrupt intellectualism. It is a hellish vision of the American educational system.

FACULTY PROFILES

We've already encountered some of Noir University's faculty, such as college professors Dr. Tuttle and Dr. Stanley, as well as prep-school master Rupert Cadell (all-boy prep academies being the major feeder schools for NU's murderous student body), but before the tour ends there are a few notable members of the faculty left for us to meet.

The standard image of a professor in film noir is that of a stuffy intellectual. See, for example, psychology professor Richard Wanley (Edward G. Robinson) in Fritz Lang's *The Woman in the Window* (1944). Happily married and content with his job giving lectures with titles like "Some Psychological Aspects of Homicide," he nevertheless longs for excitement. Then one night he meets beautiful Alice Reed (Joan Bennett) and follows her home for a drink. When a stranger (Arthur Loft) breaks into her apartment and attacks them, Wanley kills the man in the struggle. Afraid to lose his family and career to scandal, Wanley disposes of the body, but he's plagued by both guilt and a blackmailer (Dan Duryea) who knows what happened. Psychological aspects of homicide, indeed.

Other presentations of professors are more ambiguous. Edgar G. Ulmer's *Strange Illusion* (1945) opens with Dr. Vincent (Regis Toomey) waking up his student Paul (Jimmy Lydon) as the boy is screaming in his sleep. The forty-seven-year-old psychology professor and his twenty-year-old student, we learn, are staying in a cabin in the woods on an extended fishing trip. This unorthodox situation is never addressed, and the professor asks Paul not to let his disturbing dream "spoil our little outing." Odder still, when a neighbor brings them a letter the next day, Dr. Vincent quips,

Professor Charles Rankin (Orson Welles) is a Nazi mastermind in *The Stranger*.

"What are you doing, spying on us?" Although Paul has a quasi-girlfriend ("quasi" because while she seems interested in him, he is pointedly dismissive of her), his only real confidant seems to be the middle-aged academic who has nothing else to do but hang around listening to his dreams. This gay-coded relationship is notable mostly because it's presented without judgment or dark pretext. The screenplay by Adele Comandini, from an original story by Fritz Rotter, simply accepts the relationship, then gets on with the murder plot involving Paul's mother and would-be stepfather.

By contrast, the darkest vision we have of an intellectual is found in Orson Welles's *The Stranger* (1946). In the film, Welles plays secret ex-Nazi Franz Kindler, who is posing as an erudite professor named Charles Rankin at the Harper School for Boys, another noir prep school.[5] As director, Welles contrasts the all-American town of Harper against the seething evil of the Nazi in its midst. His presentation of small-town life is rendered with skill and care, while his Nazi is presented as a coldly intellectual psychopath. Sounding more than a bit like Leopold and Loeb, Rankin/Kindler expounds at one point, "The German sees himself as the innocent victim of world envy and hatred, conspired against, set upon by *inferior* peoples, *inferior* nations. He cannot admit to error, much less to wrongdoing . . ." If Welles goes over the top in his portrayal of Kindler, with bugged-out eyes and Frankenstein's monster lumber, his performance as Professor Rankin (which is, after all, a Nazi's impersonation of an American academic) is more nuanced. We can believe kids would want to take this charming intellectual's classes, and we can also believe that he could help create future Leopolds and Loebs.

And *that*, after all, is the scary part. *The Stranger* crystalizes the primary anxiety so many film noirs have about education: that it holds the potential to lead impressionable minds astray, that behind the tweed jackets and five-dollar words might lurk dangerous ideas. This fear runs deep in the American psyche, of course. It's part of the ingrained anti-intellectualism that has been at the root of extremist politics for generations. In recent years, it's given rise to conspiracy theories like QAnon and to reactionary backlashes against academic fields like Critical Race Theory and Gender Studies. But as film noir's dark visions of academia make clear, suspicions about the eggheaded elite are nothing new. ■

---

5 Although *The Stranger* is not widely regarded as one of Welles's more personal films, the filmmaker clearly patterned the Harper School on his own beloved prep academy, the Todd School for Boys in Woodstock, Illinois. There's even a flyer on the wall in one shot announcing an upcoming basketball game between Harper and Todd.

THE BIG RUB DOWN

By Brent Calderwood

MASSEURS AND MASSEUSES IN **FILM NOIR**

It's after midnight. A wounded cop-killer limps up the steps of a Manhattan brownstone with a neon sign reading "Mme. Rose Swedish Massage" and rings the bell. He's been ducking into shadows all night to dodge the police detective on his trail; now he watches through the scuffed door's glass pane as a hulking silhouette lumbers into view at the end of a shotgun hallway, switching on lights as it slowly moves forward. Finally filling the doorway, a six-foot-two, 230-pound masseuse clad in crisp white glowers down—a stare that dares the five-foot-eight stranger to talk his way inside.

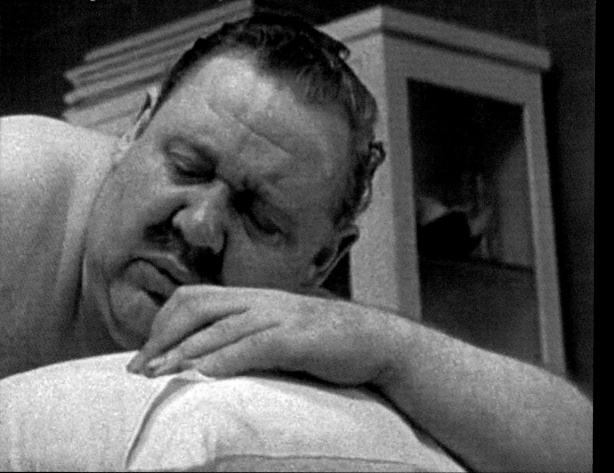

Massage parlor proprietress Rose Given (Hope Emerson) shows Martin Rome (Richard Conte) who has the upper hand in *Cry of the City*.

The movie is *Cry of the City* (1948). The man on the run is Richard Conte. And the massive masseuse is Hope Emerson, who gets one of the most sinister and masterfully lit entrances in film noir, courtesy of director Robert Siodmak and cinematographer Lloyd Ahern. For years, Hollywood mainly portrayed masseurs and masseuses—and their pampered clientele—as laughingstocks rather than cold-blooded criminals, but Emerson's scowl tells a different story. This is Dark City, where rubdowns are rarely played for humor, and where manhandling masseuses and oily masseurs ratchet up tension instead of relieving it; where a healing touch can turn to a death grip in seconds, and where crossing the threshold of a late-night massage parlor never leads to a happy ending.

Once she realizes who he is, Emerson (as massage parlor proprietress Rose Given) leads Conte's Martin Rome past UV lamps, sweat cabinets, and stacks of white towels to her private apartment where Rome, exhausted, looks for a place to lie down. "Here," she intones as she begins rubbing his shoulders. "I have the touch. It's only given to a few . . . and I waste this on fat old women who think they can lose a few pounds and be beautiful again. Fat old women who have too much money and too many jewels." As her grip tightens around Rome's throat, his suspicions are confirmed: Rose is the "mystery girl" behind the jewel theft and murder that's been pinned on him. It's the most famous scene in the movie, justly praised in 1955 by Raymond Borde and Etienne Chaumeton in the first book-length study of film noir, *Panorama du film noir américain*.[1] It's also a moment that doesn't exist in the novel.

In Henry Edward Helseth's source novel, *The Chair for Martin Rome* (1947), the character of

---

1 The authors call Rose "a real 'phallic woman,' who, with a flick of the wrists, has a 'tough guy' at her mercy" (translated by Paul Hammond in 2002).

Rose is a petite, twentyish sex worker, but when it came to the screen adaptation, massage, with its nearly naked exchanges of power and money, was a useful stand-in for topics verboten under the Motion Picture Production Code; in addition, masseurs and masseuses provided screenwriters with an ingenious alternative to voice-over narration by giving prone, vulnerable characters someone to talk to. No wonder massage scenes appear in classic noirs such as *In a Lonely Place*, *The Big Clock*, *The Big Knife*, and *Nightmare Alley*—as well as noir-stained films like *Rear Window*—even though there are no rubdowns in the books, plays, and short stories those pictures are based on.

A LIGHTER TOUCH

Before the original noir period (from 1940 to 1959), rubdowns were almost always played for laughs, starting with the 1905 silent comedy short *The Broadway Massage Parlor* up through 1939's *The Women*—in which a roomful of doughy dowagers are kneaded by loose-tongued masseuses in a what's-a-Depression luxury spa—but as movies grew darker during and especially after World War II, massage scenes became more ominous.

A notable exception to this trend is *Rear Window* (1954). In Alfred Hitchcock's thriller, based on Cornell Woolrich's 1942 short story "It Had to Be Murder," Thelma Ritter plays a worldly-wise insurance company nurse who spreads a sheet across James Stewart's daybed and slathers his back in cold massage oil ("It gives your circulation something to fight"). During her first house call, as Ritter pulls bottles of oil and rubbing alcohol from her bag, she predicts the film's plot. ("I can smell trouble right here in this apartment. First you smash your leg, then you get to lookin' out the window, see things you shouldn't see. Trouble.") At this point, Stewart doesn't suspect anyone of murder, and between his toe-to-navel leg cast and her no-nonsense mien, there's no skin-crawling tension; the only suspense to speak of is whether Stewart will stop eyeing the cuties across the courtyard and finally settle down. For "noir or not" debaters who put *Rear Window* in the "not" category—too glamorous, too funny, too Technicolor—here's one more angle: in film noir, massage recipients are usually burdened by bigger dilemmas than whether to marry Grace Kelly.

Cold comfort: Nurse Stella (Thelma Ritter) slathers Jeff (James Stewart) with cold rubbing oil in *Rear Window*.

Martha (an uncredited Ruth Gillette) comes to Laurel Gray's (Gloria Grahame) bedroom twice a week to beat her "black and blue" in *In a Lonely Place*.

TURNING THE TABLES

In *In a Lonely Place* (1950), aspiring starlet Laurel Gray's (Gloria Grahame) existential loneliness exists even before she meets tortured screenwriter Dix Steele (Humphrey Bogart). Her only confidante is Martha (Ruth Gillette), whom Laurel describes as "the only thing left of my movie career." Explaining to Dix that Martha's "about fifty" and married with a grown son—is this to quell Dix's suspicious mind or the censors?—Laurel continues, "She comes to me twice a week, beats me black and blue." When we finally meet Martha, it's in the film's lowest angle and starkest shot, the camera looking up from the edge of a massage table in Laurel's bedroom at a close-up of Grahame's face and bare shoulders; Martha, whose menacing mug floats over Laurel's left shoulder, is positioned both as predator and advising angel. But whereas *Rear Window*'s masseuse doubles as a conscience by warning against voyeurism, the butch, bulky Martha (a character not in Dorothy B. Hughes's novel) presses harder, verbalizing Laurel's subconscious worries: She condemns Dix's violence, balks at his barked request for breakfast ("What, no caviar?"), and advises Laurel to return to a safer, more transactional relationship ("We should be up on Miller Drive beside that lovely pool that Mr. Baker built for you"). When Laurel defends Dix and tells Martha to leave, Martha folds up her table with the ease of a strongman, purring, "You'll beg me to come back when you're in trouble. You will, Angel, because you don't have anybody else." Her incongruously silky voice, so similar to Laurel's, reinforces a resonance between the women that lasts even when Martha is offscreen: Laurel is on the phone with Martha before her first long conversation and fade-out kiss with Dix; later, Martha calls during the couple's engagement party, sending Dix into a rage that carries through to his final act of violence. Most importantly, this massage scene marks a narrative switch in the film from Dix's point of view to Laurel's.

Laurel's willingness to be beaten "black and blue" for her movie career was not unusual. In the name of beauty, youthfulness, and desirability, aspiring stars and starlets subjected themselves to the "beatings" of masseuses such as Hollywood's most famous, Madame Sylvia, who claimed in her 1932 tell-all, *Hollywood Undressed*, that bodies and faces could be literally molded through regular intense massage and that "the fat comes out through the pores like mashed potato through a colander."[2] One of Sylvia's clients, Gloria Swanson, conveyed this masochistic side of massage in *Sunset Boulevard* (1950) as faded silent-screen star Norma Desmond, who undergoes an intense beauty regimen to revitalize her career, including a mud rub and upper-body massage combined with electro-passive pads attached to her thighs and waist to firm and reduce the offending areas. Part of the horror of this beauty montage[3] is the audience's awareness that Norma cannot recapture the past; but although Laurel (unlike Norma Desmond) appears to have given up on stardom, it seems likely she'll continue her lesbian-coded sessions with Martha, who will call Laurel "Angel" while working her knots and slapping her butt when it's time to turn over.

ANYTHING FOR THE BOSS

Martha isn't the only hyperattentive rubdown artist in noir. In a host of other noir entries, male massage professionals (and amateurs) rub their bosses with varying degrees of homoerotic vim (a marked departure from earlier crime dramas such as *Marked Woman* [1937] and *Racket Busters* [1938], in which discreetly draped gang bosses get massages as a straightforward display of wealth and power[4]). But whereas female clients' massages were about reduction and punishment, men's massages were generally gentler, aimed at soothing stress after workdays or workouts.

In *The Big Clock* (1948), Harry Morgan plays Bill, a seemingly mute, black-suited servant and bodyguard of press baron Earl Janoth (Charles Laughton) who attends to his boss's every need—this includes stripping to his white undershirt and providing massage services in a tiled rubdown room.[5] As Bill warms up rubbing alcohol in his hands and begins to knead his boss's ample flesh, Janoth hints that Bill should shoot the suspected murderer they're looking for on sight, and then they can doctor a posthumous confession letter. As Janoth unspools the plan, Bill stares ahead intently, his strokes slowing to a caress as he contemplates the pleasure of getting to use his gun. The insertion of such heavy-handed homosexual subtext is a clever, creepy solution to the Production Code–required redaction of actual homosexual text in the book: In Kenneth Fearing's *The Big Clock* (1946), Janoth accuses his girlfriend of lesbian promiscuity, and when she counters that he is having a relationship with his "fairy gorilla" of a business partner, Janoth kills her in a blind rage. Bill, on the other hand, is merely Janoth's chauffeur in the novel and never lays a finger on him.

The Big Knife (1955) goes a step further by inventing not just a scene but a character who doesn't exist in its source material, the Clifford Odets play of the same name from 1949. Screenwriter James Poe adds a backyard rubdown scene to the one-room play, along with a boxing trainer, Mickey (Nick Dennis), who helps flesh out movie-star protagonist Charlie Castle's (Jack Palance) Hollywood milieu. After a sparring session, Mickey massages Charlie on a rubdown table while Charlie's agent,

---

2   Sylvia's competitor, the zaftig Louise Long, gave "beatings" to clients including Marlene Dietrich, Lana Turner, and Coleen Gray; she may have been the direct inspiration for Martha, according to Gray ("Ask Eddie," Film Noir Foundation, May 12, 2022).
3   Horror is the word. Compare a similar montage in Karl Freund's 1935 chiller *Mad Love*, in which massage and electro-stimulation are used to ensure a successful transplantation when an injured pianist is given the hands of a recently executed knife-thrower.
4   One of the few noirs with an uncomplicated massage is *I Walk Alone* (1947), where postwar nightclub owner Kirk Douglas is briefly shown getting a rubdown; it telegraphs the power and wealth he accumulated during his own prewar gangster past—plus it's an excuse to show audiences a shirtless Douglas.
5   The part seems tailor-made for Morgan, who played a mute character in *Moonrise* (1948) and a shifty steam room attendant in *Somewhere in the Night* (1946).

Massage interruptus: Dana Andrews walks in on Neville Brand (center) giving his gang boss, Gary Merrill, a rubdown in *Where the Sidewalk Ends*.

Nat (Everett Sloane), delivers extended exposition about his client's career problems; this dialogue is accompanied by one of the most thorough massages in noir, with Nick applying oil and then alcohol to his boss's athletic chest, back, shoulders, arms, and legs. When Charlie gets riled by Nat and raises himself off the table, Mickey pulls his boss into a clinch/hug, whispering in his ear, "Is there anything a Greek can do?" Mickey's puppyish attention—including calling Charlie "Sweetheart"—blurs the line between homosocial and homoerotic; in the end, Mickey is the most loyal of Charlie's entourage of hangers-on, but his altruism is diluted by his cloying affection, and by his being an employee.

In a final example of subtly sexualized rubdown service, *Where the Sidewalk Ends* (1950) includes a scene in a Turkish bath in which gang boss Gary Merrill lies supine on a massage table having his thigh rubbed by his tall, young henchman (Neville Brand). Brand (like Morgan in *The Big Clock*) is stripped down to his undershirt and suit pants, working away despite the presence of two bath attendants in their signature white uniforms; this intimacy intimates that Merrill's character fits into the noir tradition of crime bosses whose gunmen are also devoted gunsels (*The Maltese Falcon*, *The Big Combo*, *The Lineup*).

HEAT TREATMENTS

Where the Sidewalk Ends is just one of the dozen or so noirs featuring Turkish baths—no surprise since mid-century Turkish baths were often connected to other Dark City locales such as boxing gyms, YMCA-style rooming houses, and urban amusement zones. A scaled-down version of Muslim hammams, Turkish baths offered three main services: steam room, massage (provided by "rubbers"[6]), and

---

[6] "Rubber" continued to be used as unisex slang for masseurs and masseuses, especially in newspapers, into the mid-century and occasionally to this day. Witness this punning society item about wartime resource scarcity: "[An LA local] reports that he got a Turkish bath and had to wait an hour for a rubdown, because of the rubber shortage" (*Los Angeles Times*, April 25, 1942).

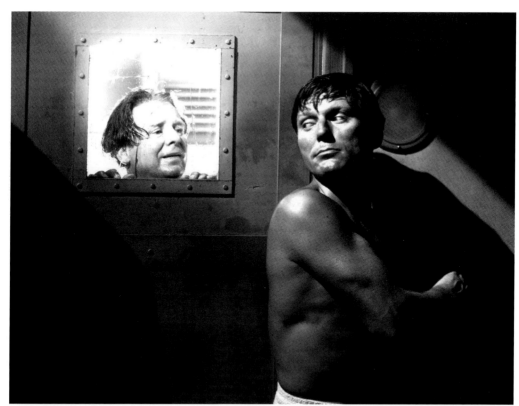
Charles McGraw in *T-Men* wasn't the first noir killer to lock a chump (Wallace Ford) in a steam room, but he was definitely the scariest.

bathing in pools, tubs, or showers. All the rage in Victorian England, Turkish baths made their way to New York in 1863 and had arrived in Los Angeles by the 1880s. They were such a hit that six decades later in *T-Men* (1947), when titular Treasury man Dennis O'Keefe thumbs through the Los Angeles Classified Telephone Directory under "Baths" (to track down a steam-freak counterfeiter), there are sixty establishments, from Ali Baba to Young's, offering massages with a range of adjectives: "Swedish," "orthopedic," "reducing," "vibratory," "expert," and "scientific"—the last term being especially popular to offset public concerns that men's bathhouses were hotbeds of illicit sexual conduct.[7]

After O'Keefe's foray in *T-Men*, he returned to a Turkish bath in *Abandoned* (1949), where he's an undercover newspaperman getting rubbed down by a cagey masseur named Doc Tilson (Bruce Hamilton) who's connected to a baby-adoption racket; the "Doc" moniker implies he offers scientific massages, but it may also relate to obstetric skills.

On the lighter side of massages in Turkish baths, George Macready appears in *The Missing Juror* (1944) as a poetry-reciting client of masseur Mike Mazurki. Despite Macready's penchant for Oscar Wilde, which he passes along to Mazurki, the scene's goofiness—as well as the presence of an earnest news reporter played by Jim Bannon—throws cold water on any sexual subtext, and the noir tone is restored when, moments later, Macready locks Bannon in the steam room and turns the valve to full blast.[8]

---

7   After finding the counterfeiter, O'Keefe deadpans to his fellow T-man, "Did you ever spend ten days in a Turkish bath looking for a man? Don't."

8   Locked, stifling steam rooms appeared later in *T-Men* and *Stopover Tokyo* (1957). Steam rooms and Turkish baths also figure in *When Strangers Marry* (1944), *Somewhere in the Night*, *They Won't Believe Me*, *House of Strangers* (1949), *The Phenix City Story* (1955), *The Lineup* (1958), and *The Case Against Brooklyn* (1958). In addition, there is a Turkish bath next door to the Ringside Café in *The Set-Up* and an overheated sweat cabinet in 1964's *The Killers*.

PUMMELED: A RUNDOWN OF BOXING RUBDOWNS

The rubdown table is the literal center of the dressing room in scores of boxing movies. It's where fighters sit in trunks and towels while deals are struck between trainers, managers, and promoters; and where they take power naps and get post-match patch-ups. The rubdown table is where boxers get their actual rubdowns, too—oil, cocoa butter, or Vaseline before the fight to show off muscles and deflect blows, wintergreen rubbing alcohol afterward to soothe sore bodies.

Early in Stanley Kubrick's *Killer's Kiss* (1955), welterweight Davey Gordon's trainer preps his man for a bout, rubbing oil on his chest, back, and arms with documentary detail, down to massaging his face to loosen up his glass jaw and the post-dubbed sounds of oil slathered on skin and chest hair. It's a scene reminiscent of Kubrick's earlier short documentary, *Day of the Fight* (1951), in which middleweight Walter Cartier's twin brother rubs petroleum jelly on Walter's face and chest before he heads into the ring.

It's no surprise that **The Set-Up** (1949), widely considered the greatest of all boxing noirs, features the most detailed and multipurpose use of the rubdown table as a stable of ham-and-eggers prepare for their bouts and come back bruised and bloodied. Before one fighter's turn, it's a bed for a quick rest; after another's it's an exam table for a concerned doctor. In the most extended rubdown, dressing-room attendant Gus (Wallace Ford) applies cocoa butter to the back, chest, and shoulders of Luther Hawkins, the African American boxer played by James Edwards (director Robert Wise had hoped Edwards would portray the protagonist in keeping with the source material, Joseph Moncure March's book-length poem about an aging Black boxer, but white actor Robert Ryan was ultimately cast in the lead role); then Gus rubs Luther's legs with alcohol while the fighter dreams of bigger matches in bigger cities. Tellingly, Stoker Thompson (Ryan), who's been set up by his manager to take a fall, is virtually ignored after his first perfunctory rubdown; when he wins and returns alone to the dressing room, it's empty except for Gus and his assistant, but before they can treat Stoker, he's surrounded by heavies ready to extract revenge.

The slightly corny B noir **Breakdown** (1952), a starring vehicle for Ann Richards (who played Burt Lancaster's sleuthing ex in *Sorry, Wrong Number*), focuses on a manager's almost obsessive worry that his fighter will get knocked out, wreck his face, or go permanently punchy. The blandly handsome fighter spends much of the film in the dressing room getting rubbed down or checked for injuries; his girlfriend (Richards) is far less worried and loves the gym with its "smell of wintergreen and alcohol and so much activity."

The Brit noir **Bad Blonde** (1953)—an engaging rip-off of *The Postman Always Rings Twice* transported from the California coast to Stratford-upon-Avon—is unusual in bringing the female gaze front and center to a boxing picture and flying under the radar of US censors. When bad blonde Barbara Payton first sees beefy blond Tony Wright (who was being groomed for sex-symbol stardom) in the ring, the POV camera lingers on his satin trunks; when the fight is over, Payton, on the arm of her soon-to-be-knocked-off husband, enters the back room while Wright is getting his post-win massage. It's a hoot to see her lick her lips and greedily size him up in his white towel with the same gusto John Garfield gave to Lana Turner in *Bad Blonde*'s more famous inspiration.

—*Brent Calderwood*

RUDE AWAKENINGS

As common as Turkish baths and massage services were in working- and middle-class athletic clubs, they were also a staple of well-heeled gentlemen's clubs and hotels. In *They Won't Believe Me* (1947), Robert Young gets a morning rubdown at his LA men's club, but is jolted from his post-massage bliss by a page phone call from a woman purporting to be the mistress whose death he covered up. It's a turning point that sets in motion the murder trial that serves as the film's framing device.

An even more dramatic turning point occurs in *Nightmare Alley* (1947). Stanton Carlisle (Tyrone Power) receives a late-night hotel-room massage to help him fall asleep after performing his mentalist act downstairs in the famous Spode Room at Chicago's Sherman House Hotel, but the smell of the masseur's rubbing alcohol sends Stan flashing back to the wood alcohol he had more-or-less accidentally given to his mentor, Pete Krumbein (Ian Keith), on the night Pete died; sense memory gives way to sound as Stan hears the screams of the carnival geek who was fiending for his promised hooch on the same deadly night. The moment sets the third act in motion, as Stan attempts to exorcise his demons by revealing the secret of Pete's death to psychiatrist Dr. Lilith Ritter (Helen Walker), giving her the ammunition she needs to swindle Stan and send him on his own nosedive into dipsomania and geekdom. The crucial massage scene, with its large glass bottle of clear rubbing alcohol—an identical triplet of the bottles of liquor and wood alcohol Stan had mixed up—draws a throughline from the first act to the denouement and is just one of countless dialogue, character, and image parallels screenwriter Jules Furthman concocted to lend cinematic structure to William Lindsay Gresham's multi-POV, complexly episodic 1946 novel.[9]

FINISHING STROKES

As the Production Code began to loosen at the end of the 1950s, massage all but vanished as a plot point or coded substitute for sex and violence; instead, massage became a means to show sex and violence in new and more explicit ways.

The James Bond franchise in particular was a reliable purveyor of massage scenes. *Goldfinger* (1964), *Thunderball* (1965), and *You Only Live Twice* (1967) all used massage to show off Sean Connery's hirsute physique and seduction techniques.[10] And in *The Godfather* (1972), an assassin memorably shoots a bespectacled mobster in the eye while he is getting a rubdown, flooding his glasses with blood. By the 1980s, with the advent of home video, massage became a common theme for instructional videos and, of course, porn. But the arrival of VHS and newer formats also spawned an ongoing renaissance of appreciation and viewership for classic noir, which remains to this day the creative climax of massage's use in films with actual plots. ■

---

9 Despite Power's efforts to leave behind his swashbuckler roles, the massage scene was also an opportunity for 20th Century-Fox to show off their asset's physical assets before he becomes fully deglamorized.

10 Italian posters for *Thunderball* made Connery's massage a particular selling point, including suggestive positioning of the 007 gun logo.

THE SMALL-TOWN CHARMS OF *COVER UP*

By Bob Sassone

The "Christmas noir" is a reliable subgenre. Maybe it's the look of beauty and mystery you get when you put falling white snow against the background of darkness and shadow, or the way the cheeriness of the holiday smashes into the coldness of murder that makes these films so effective.

There's *Blast of Silence* (1961), the low-budget but marvelously intense hit-man flick written and directed by its star, Allen Baron; *Lady in the Lake* (1947), the first-person-camera mystery with Robert Montgomery as Raymond Chandler's Philip Marlowe; the Mike Hammer 3D action noir *I, the Jury* (1953); *Cash on Demand* (1961), the criminally underseen British bank heist film with Peter Cushing; the neo-noir *L.A. Confidential* (1997); and *Christmas Holiday* (1944), the movie where Gene Kelly kills a guy and doesn't dance. If we're being generous with the definition, we can include *The Thin Man* (from 1934 and too early to be a true noir, though the style is there) and *It's a Wonderful Life* (1946), if only for the dark, surreal "Pottersville" section, which is more noir than many movies labeled as such.

But the one that screams Christmas to me is *Cover Up* (1949), a modest "light noir" that's not only one of the great underrated mysteries but also one of the most underrated films of all time, period.

Cover Up was the first of three films from Dennis O'Keefe's production company, Strand Productions. The other two, *A Kiss for Corliss* (with Shirley Temple and David Niven) and *Without Honor* (with Bruce Bennett, Laraine Day, Dane Clark, and Agnes Moorehead) were also released in 1949. But *Cover Up* is the standout, a little film with a few big tricks up its sleeve.

Sam Donovan (O'Keefe) is the most honest insurance man in the world, coming to the small Midwestern town of Cleberg to confirm that one of his company's policyholders, Roger Phillips, really did commit suicide. The fact that a murder would double the amount of money they have to pay the beneficiary doesn't seem to bother Donovan or his boss, who explains that being an honest insurance company would be great for publicity—and besides, maybe the beneficiary committed the murder. (This isn't entirely convincing, but you just go with it.)

I've seen *Cover Up* a dozen times, and it took all twelve for me to figure out why it appeals to me so much. One reason is I'm a sucker for holiday movies—*It's a Wonderful Life* and *Miracle on 34th Street* (1947) are my two favorite films—and the other is I deeply love *Perry Mason* (1957–66) and *Murder, She Wrote* (1984–96). *Cover Up* is structured like those mysteries. Someone dies, and then one by one we meet the suspects and learn their secrets, leaving the hero to figure out whodunnit and whydunit. With a running time of less than 85 minutes, *Cover Up* plays like an extended episode of one of those shows.

Was it the beneficiary, Margaret Baker (a pre–Folger's Coffee commercial Virginia Christine), the

Dennis O'Keefe (pictured here with Barbara Britton) cowrote this yuletide noir under the name Jonathan Rix, and his company produced the film.

dead man's niece? Was it her husband, Frank (Russell Armes), who wasn't where he said he was at the time of Phillips's death? Was it Mr. Abbey (Paul E. Burns), the jeweler who found the body, or Hilda (Doro Merande), the sarcastic, nosy housekeeper? Or maybe it was the calm, wise Sheriff Best (William Bendix), who banters with Donovan in several well-written scenes but is unhelpful when it comes to the gun used in the "suicide" (it disappeared!).

It couldn't be Anita (Barbara Britton), could it? She's the woman Donovan meets on the bus to Cleberg and instantly falls in love with. Nah, they make it clear she's not under suspicion—but she does try to cover up for the person who might be the number one suspect: her banker father, Mr. Weatherby (Art Baker), who walks around town in a big fur coat that becomes a big part of the plot.

This cast of varied small-town characters is why *Cover Up* also reminds me of *The Andy Griffith Show* (1960–68). Just replace Sheriff Taylor with Sheriff Best, and make the plot about the possible murder of a man the whole town hated instead of a pickle-making contest. Come to think of it, Mayberry also had a man everyone hated, department store owner Ben Weaver. *Cover Up* even has a bumbling deputy with slicked-back hair who's a little too quick with his gun. All that's missing is a barber and a town drunk—though I'm sure those people exist in Cleberg, we just don't see them.

Every single one of these people has a secret. Whenever Donovan leaves after talking to one of them, they have a concerned look on their face, as if they're afraid that he's going to figure out what happened.

I know, I know, this happens in every movie and TV show like this—especially the aforementioned *Perry Mason* and *Murder, She Wrote*—so you're probably wondering what makes *Cover Up* stand out from every other low-budget mystery. Why am I even writing about it and imploring you to watch it on TCM or buy it (it's now on Blu-ray from Kino Lorber)?

All right, I'll tell you, right after I put in big, bold letters: **SPOILER ALERT**.

Cover Up is the only film noir and the only murder mystery I've seen where we not only never meet the victim, *we never even meet the killer*. We learn their name, but they're never shown!

Every time I watch the film I wonder was this a choice by the writers (the screenplay was cowritten by O'Keefe—credited as Jonathan Rix—and Jerome Odlum, with additional dialogue by Francis Swann and Lawrence Kimble) to make it quirky and interesting, or was it dictated by the small budget? There's no way to know from the film itself, so I'll conclude that the filmmakers wanted to create a way for the film to stand out, to throw viewers off and have clues that turn up late in the movie reveal more about those two characters. Well, at least more about the person who committed the crime—we never learn much about the victim except no one liked him.

This story decision isn't the only odd thing about the movie. The weirdness starts with the film's poster, which shows Bendix drawing his gun (he draws his pipe a lot but never his gun), O'Keefe drawing his (he only does it to fire a bullet into a pile of newspapers), and a dead body on the floor (again, we never see the victim). There's no murder depicted on-screen, there's no violent flashback, and there's hardly any action at all.

This probably all sounds ridiculous on paper. They never show the murderer *or* the victim? How does that even work? What bad plotting! How lazy! It's neither of those things. In fact, you don't notice not seeing these characters because a) there are already many characters to get to know and b) when you do realize it, it kinda makes you smile.

The whole movie makes me smile, actually. I want to live in Cleberg. Yes, there's a murder, but at the end we find out that it's a great place to live. The people are nice, there's a town square where the whole town shows up to watch the Christmas tree lighting, and when a beloved member of the community dies of a heart attack, you believe they cared about him.

And even though it's a really small town, it has *two* movie theaters, right across the street from each other!

Director Alfred E. Green, whose long career includes *The Gracie Allen Murder Case* (1939), *The Jackie Robinson Story* (1950), and *Invasion, U.S.A.* (1952), doesn't show off, letting the film amble along at its own pace, with an occasional neat camera angle or reveal; there's a clever scene where Britton hides from another character behind a door, and we see her reflection but the person she's hiding from doesn't. At once leisurely and loose as well as tight and neat, it's the type of realistic film where you simply forget its flaws.

Early in the movie we see that the Weatherby family has already put up their decorated Christmas tree—and then, late in the movie, the family decorates it again. In a bigger-budget film that bit of carelessness might stick out like an ugly Christmas sweater, but here you don't care.

I've already spoiled a lot, so I won't reveal how the movie ends. Let's just say that as the characters walk out the front door of the home where the murder was committed and you see the snow falling in the streetlights knowing that the murder has been solved, you're going to want to live in Cleberg, too. I don't know how morally sound the main character's actions are at the end, but they're deeply satisfying.

If you're like most people, your usual yuletide fare includes *White Christmas* (1954), *The Bishop's Wife* (1947), and *Christmas in Connecticut* (1945). Maybe you even watch those Hallmark/Lifetime movies where a driven female executive goes to a town to close down a factory but ends up falling in love with the local handyman who happens to be named "Nick" or "Kris." And you love TV specials like *Rudolph the Red-Nosed Reindeer* (1964) and *A Charlie Brown Christmas* (1965), too. Add *Cover Up* to the list. I hope it's shown more and more in November and December, to the point where it becomes as annual a tradition as the Macy's Thanksgiving Day Parade and fighting over a discounted toaster on Black Friday.

And to think that the producers wanted to drop the Christmas setting, saying it was inappropriate for a murder mystery. Let's be thankful O'Keefe stood his ground—he understood something his fellow producers didn't—and insisted that they keep it a Christmas film. One that works as both a mystery and a feel-good holiday film. Pulling off that combo is the film's neatest trick of all. ■

Horror Films
NOIR DIRECTORS

By Sharon Knolle

Many of the European émigré directors who helped to create the Expressionist-inspired noir mood and style—German expats Robert Siodmak and John Brahm, Austrian Edgar G. Ulmer, and Jacques Tourneur, the son of French director Maurice Tourneur—first paid their Hollywood dues in the far less-respected realm of horror. And many were game changers for the genre: along with producer Val Lewton, Tourneur is widely credited with creating cinema's first jump scare in *Cat People* (1942). The voyeuristic point-of-view shots in Siodmak's Gothic thriller *The Spiral Staircase* (1946) are often cited as a key influence on slasher films. (Both films were shot by Academy Award–nominated master cinematographer Nicholas Musuraca.) It can be difficult to draw the line where noir ends and horror begins. Both genres are concerned with shadowy figures, unseen threats, madness, murder, and a suffocating sense of dread and doom.

Tourneur would be best remembered today as a horror director for making such haunting classics as *The Leopard Man* (1943) and *I Walked with a Zombie* (1943) under the aegis of the legendary Lewton, had he not also gone on to direct perhaps the greatest film noir in history, *Out of the Past* (1947), as well as the underrated *Nightfall* (1956).

Cat People, the debut film from Lewton's horror unit at RKO, was a surprise hit that ushered in one of the most acclaimed run of fright films produced by any studio outside of monster mecca Universal. When Tourneur was promoted to A films, Lewton tapped his assistants Robert Wise and Mark Robson, each of whom would go on to direct their own entries in the noir canon.

The genius of Lewton—who wrote or rewrote all the films he produced—was to suggest something terrible in the shadows while rarely showing it. This eerily effective approach was never more poetically articulated than in the famous scene in *Cat People* where Alice (Jane Randolph), romantic rival to troubled Serbian immigrant Irena (Simone Simon), is followed at night by a stalker she never actually sees. As Alice becomes increasingly unnerved, she and the audience brace for the deadly leap of the panther Irena has presumably become in her jealousy. Instead, a city bus screeches to a startling halt in front of Alice, providing both a momentary shock and a break in the tension, which only builds again when Alice takes a terrifying dip in a dark swimming pool and every sound is amplified into the cry of an angry jungle cat.

A bizarre childhood experience of Tourneur's led him to recreate the paralyzing feeling of fright he felt as a young boy. In Chris Fujiwara's biography *Jacques Tourneur: The Cinema of Nightfall* (1998), the director describes how he was sent to gather his Christmas presents alone from his father's "big, mysterious" art studio. "There was a very long corridor, completely black, and I could make out in the distance the white spots that were my presents," Tourneur said. "I walked forward all alone,

Jacques Tourneur's *Cat People* subtly suggests that Simone Simon's femme fatale Irena really can turn into a deadly panther.

torn between desire for the toys and a fear that almost made me faint, especially as the toys in their packages started to take on a phantom-like appearance." He also recounted, "If I hadn't been a good boy, my parents would send the maid into the cupboard. In there she shook a bowler hat, while my parents said, 'It's the Thunderman.' That's the source of one of my obsessions: to suddenly introduce inexplicable things into a shot, like the hand on the banisters in *Night of the Demon*, which disappears in the reverse shot."

Tourneur recaptured the sense of a waking nightmare in 1957's *Night of the Demon*, but was saddled with Hal E. Chester, an interfering producer who insisted on showing the demon of the film's title. This serious flaw nevertheless does not ruin the effective chills in the tale of skeptical American professor John Holden (Dana Andrews), who cannot debunk the all-too-true horrors conjured by Julian Karswell (Niall MacGinnis), the leader of a satanic cult. *Night of the Demon* features one of the most effective jump scares of the genre: When Holden sneaks into Karswell's house by night, presuming it to be empty, the camera pulls back to reveal a hand suddenly appearing on the stairway railing. And then, in a shot from the bottom of the stairs, the hand is gone . . . and we see no one is there at all.

Tourneur later dismissed *The Leopard Man*, his second movie with Lewton, as "neither fish nor fowl." But as director William Friedkin noted in a DVD commentary, the film is decidedly both horror and noir, and more: "It's a horror film, to a great extent, and a film about the mystery of fate." The existential theme is presented just as strongly as in any film noir where the fallen hero rails against "bad luck" while tightening his own noose. But is it bad luck or the hand of fate at work in both genres? Early on in *The Leopard Man*, the character later revealed to be the killer muses that you can't

Jean Brooks plays nightclub entertainer Kiki in Tourneur's *The Leopard Man*; her boyfriend (Dennis O'Keefe) hires a black leopard for her act with disastrous consequences.

Professor John Holden's (Dana Andrews) skepticism is no match for the black magic conjured by Dr. Julian Karswell (Niall MacGinnis) in *Curse of the Demon*.

fight your destiny. Referring to a ball floating atop a pulsing outdoor fountain, he says, "We know as little about the forces that move us, that move the world around us, as that empty ball, as the water that pushes it, that lets it fall and catches it again."

Referring to the film's human killer, whose motives are never explained, Friedkin said, "This was of course influenced by Fritz Lang's *M*, where a psychotic killer has no control over himself . . . we never know why, it's simply a compulsion." As psychiatrist Dr. Judd (Tom Conway) tells Irena in *Cat People*, "There is, in some cases, a psychic need to loose evil upon the world," a sentiment that proves prophetic as a dying Irena returns to the zoo to free the panther that so intrigued her.

"These films lurk in the imagination where night terrors occur," Friedkin said of Tourneur's films with Lewton. "They have the logic or the illogic of nightmares. They have elements of surrealism. Things that happen within them are inexplicable."

While Lewton's influence is evident in all the films he oversaw, Tourneur's subtle use of shadow and light, and the motif of lines and bars caging Irena as surely as the panther at the zoo, continued into his noir films. When an emboldened Irena is kissed by Dr. Judd, he triggers the predatory cat within. We never actually see her transform; the camera pans away to the wall and the battle—which leaves the psychiatrist dead and Irena mortally wounded—plays out in silhouette, just as Tourneur and Musuraca would stage the fist fight between Robert Mitchum's detective and his former partner in *Out of the Past*.

Robert Siodmak, one of the only filmmakers to receive a Best Director Oscar nomination for a noir title (the Ernest Hemingway–based *The Killers* [1946]), is also credited for an innovation that would

Dorothy McGuire stars as a mute woman targeted by a psychotic killer in Robert Siodmak's *The Spiral Staircase*.

shape horror films decades later. The same year as *The Killers*, he directed *The Spiral Staircase*, set in 1916 New England in a spooky old house on a stormy night. Although the movie is widely embraced as a noir, it's also considered a key precursor to slasher and *giallo* films. It features point-of-view shots as the killer stalks and murders his victims, his identity unrevealed until the finale.

In Musuraca's close-ups, Siodmak himself stood in for the killer obsessed with ridding the world of "weak" women with physical handicaps. The director placing the camera (and the audience) in the killer's shoes was a technique later used by Alfred Hitchcock in *Psycho* (1960) for the same purpose, to conceal who the killer is until the final, shocking moment.

Horror gave Siodmak his big break in Hollywood. When he was on a $150-a-week contract at Universal, he reluctantly took on the Lon Chaney Jr. vehicle *Son of Dracula* (1943). His wife persuaded him to take the job, thinking it could boost his career, and she was right: three days into shooting, Siodmak was offered a seven-year contract at the studio. The film, in which Chaney's "Count Alucard" has heiress Katherine Caldwell (Louise Allbritton) inexplicably under his spell, was based on a story by his brother Curt Siodmak, who had already made his mark crafting the rich mythology of the werewolf in Universal's horror classic *The Wolf Man* (1941).

In a 1959 *Sight & Sound* interview, Robert Siodmak called the *Son of Dracula* script—written by Eric Taylor, who also penned the scripts for *The Black Cat* (1941) starring Basil Rathbone and Bela Lugosi, and the 1943 version of *Phantom of the Opera*—"terrible . . . it had been knocked together in a few days." Curt, who also wrote *I Walked with a Zombie* for Lewton, told *Starlog* magazine in 1990 that the movie "became a classic through Robert's handling of light and shadow. He was wonderful on mood, characterization, atmosphere, the psychology. He could make marvelous scenes."

While *Son of Dracula* bears little resemblance to Robert's later entries in the noir pantheon—

In Brahm's *Hangover Square*, Cregar's composer character is duped by dance-hall dame Linda Darnell, who doesn't realize he's prone to homicidal fugue states.

Laird Cregar as a man suspected of being Jack the Ripper in John Brahm's period thriller *The Lodger*.

which include *Phantom Lady* (1944), *The Dark Mirror* (1946), *Cry of the City* (1948), and *Criss Cross* (1949)—the film's apparent damsel in distress, Katherine, is revealed to be a calculating femme fatale. Instead of angling for the loot from a payroll robbery, as Kitty (Ava Gardner) does in *The Killers*, the scheming, seductive Katherine seeks eternal life as a vampire. The pawn in her game is not a dumb former boxer, but Dracula himself.

Nearly all of John Brahm's films feature someone in the grip of an all-consuming passion. In *The Lodger* (1944) and *Hangover Square* (1945), the main characters (both played by Laird Cregar) are driven to kill women, while in his noir *The Locket* (1946), antiheroine Nancy (Laraine Day) is compelled to steal jewels because of a childhood incident where she was falsely accused of purloining the title token. Despite their crimes, we have sympathy for these doomed creatures who seem to know not what they do.

In *The Lodger*, the scene where Cregar's Mr. Slade seethes with hatred and barely restrained violence as Kitty Langley (Merle Oberon) dances the cancan might have been the blueprint for the one in *The Night of the Hunter* (1955) where Harry Powell (Robert Mitchum) so strongly disapproves of a burlesque dancer that he flicks a knife open in his pocket, tearing his jacket. Tension mounts as the family housing Slade begins to suspect he is Jack the Ripper. The film gives the Ripper a motive for his hideous murders: his idealized late brother was betrayed by an actress, and therefore Slade must kill all duplicitous women of the stage.

In *Hangover Square*, Cregar's composer George Bone is almost blameless, as he enters a dissociative fugue state whenever he hears a discordant sound. He later wakens to find himself bloodied, with a dim memory of having committed murder. He's a tragic figure, for he has no control over the crimes he commits while in this condition, which include stabbing an antique dealer and strangling the woman who romanced him only for his songs. A man gripped by forces he cannot control bears a strong resemblance to *The Wolf Man*, in which Lawrence Talbot (Lon Chaney Jr.) transforms into a werewolf and kills when the moon is full, and noirs such as *Black Angel* (1946), in which alcoholic Dan Duryea cannot be sure if he's a murderer or not after a booze-induced blackout. The words fortune teller Maleva (Maria Ouspenskaya) pronounces over the cursed Talbot could just as well apply to the poor, haunted George: "The way you walked was thorny, through no fault of your own. But as the rain enters the soil, the river enters the sea, so tears run to a predestined end." Cregar's easily suggestible composer also has much in common with William Bendix's wounded naval officer Buzz Wanchek in *The Blue Dahlia* (1946). A metal plate in his head sends Buzz into a rage whenever he hears loud music. Screenwriter Raymond Chandler intended for the hair-trigger vet to be the villain who snaps and kills Alan Ladd's wife in the film, until the Navy objected to having a serviceman as a murderer, and a nosy hotel detective became the fall guy instead.

Likewise, poor mixed-up Nancy in Brahm's *The Locket* seems to have no control over her pathological behavior, even when it leads to murder. She cheerfully denies all accusations as she truly seems to have no knowledge of them—until the film's finale, when she has a complete mental breakdown upon finally receiving the cherished locket she was denied as a girl. The sense of a Greek tragedy is underlined by Nancy's romance with painter Norman (Robert Mitchum), who paints her as seer Cassandra. Only he is the real Cassandra in the film, warning everyone about her evil ways and watching helplessly as another man falls under Nancy's spell.

In 1979, Brahm granted his last interview to David Del Valle, who asked him if famed German studio UFA had influenced his films. "My early years were spent in such a way that the dark atmosphere came naturally," Brahm said. "My uncle, Otto Brahm, was very respected in Germany as a theatrical producer around the turn of the century, and through him, as a boy, I saw productions of *Faust* and *Die Niebelungen*. I was fascinated with the dark and fantastic, even as a child; the *Puppenspielen* (puppet shows) that came to town would always play Faust and the Devil."

Brahm went on to lend his uncanny sensibility to classic episodes of *The Alfred Hitchcock Hour* (1962–65) and *The Twilight Zone* (1959–64), including the latter's unforgettable "Judgment Night"

Robert Mitchum lives to regret embracing a mentally ill Laraine Day in *The Locket*.

Bela Lugosi and Boris Karloff are deadly adversaries in Edgar G. Ulmer's horror masterpiece *The Black Cat*.

(1959), in which a man (Nehemiah Persoff) relives the same night over and over as one of several people killed by a U-boat attack on a passenger ship, only to realize that he is the Nazi captain who ordered the strike.

Ulmer came to Hollywood in 1926 to assist with the art direction on F.W. Murnau's *Sunrise* (1927). The second US film he directed was the still-shocking horror classic *The Black Cat* (1934) for Universal, which pitted Satanist Hjalmar Poelzig (Boris Karloff) against vengeance-hungry psychiatrist Vitus Werdegast (Bela Lugosi). Even in pre-Code Hollywood, Ulmer couldn't show Lugosi actually skinning his archrival alive at the film's end. Instead, the camera pans away to Karloff's manacled hands and their shadows on the wall, a subtlety of storytelling that cannot have been lost on Lewton.

Werdegast tries to stop Poelzig from sacrificing the newlywed bride who has become a pawn in their game, but in the confusion Werdegast is shot by the groom. As the two innocents make their escape, Werdegast says, "You fool, I was only trying to help you," but is resigned to his death, as if expecting it. With grim satisfaction, he takes his mortal enemy with him as flips the switch detonating the explosives that bring down Poelzig's great stone house.

Ulmer made the Parisian period thriller *Bluebeard* (1944) in a mere six days, a calculated move by Poverty Row studio Producers Releasing Corporation to cash in on the success of *The Lodger*. John Carradine stars as puppeteer Gaston Morell, who has abandoned his first love of painting as he is impelled to kill the women who model for him.

If the stunning minimalist architecture in *The Black Cat* was part of his Bauhaus period, this serial-killer drama was "very much influenced at the time by Grand Guignol—which took me twenty years to get out of my system!" Ulmer said of the film, which takes its inspiration from the ghoulish theater that specialized in the same macabre type of entertainment shown in Karl Freund's *Mad Love* (1935).

Heroine Lucille (Jean Parker) is introduced to Morell at his elaborately staged puppet show of Faust, the medieval legend of a man who makes a deal with the devil. The scene, which runs nearly five minutes, cannot help but remind cineastes that Ulmer worked with Murnau on his 1926 silent film based on the Goethe morality tale.

The brooding Morell falls in love with Lucille, and commissions her to design costumes for his marionettes. Although there is a serial killer loose, Lucille implicitly trusts the charming but melancholy Morell. It's almost too late when she realizes that he is not a sensitive artist but a man who relives romantic disappointment through murder.

In his biography *Edgar G. Ulmer: A Filmmaker at the Margins* (2014), Noah Isenberg sees a parallel between filmmaker and subject for, as Ulmer once said, "I really am looking for absolution for all the things I had to do for money's sake."

Ulmer was first announced as the director of *Bluebeard* for Universal in 1934—until he began an affair with the wife of studio head Carl Laemmle's nephew. He was banned from all the major Hollywood studios, but continued making impressive B movies on shoestring budgets.

If the director identified with his strange strangler in *Bluebeard*, he surely saw himself in the sad sack main character of his 1945 noir *Detour*, the film Roger Ebert called "an embodiment of the guilty soul of film noir." Tom Neal's unemployed musician Al crosses paths with Ann Savage's Vera, a hitchhiker who sends his already hard-luck life into a dead-end spiral. At the film's close, Al sits in a roadside diner in a state of limbo, certain he'll be pinched sooner or later for the two murders on his tab.

"Someday a car will stop to pick me up that I never thumbed," he says in voiceover as he trudges down a lonely road, a highway patrol car stopping to pick him up exactly as he'd predicted. "Yes. Fate, or some mysterious force, can put the finger on you or me for no good reason at all." It's a prophetic line that could serve as a mantra for all of noir—and for many horror films. ∎

PUNK, NOIR, AND THE MOON UPSTAIRS

By Chris D.

It starts as friend, then friendly lover / and ends as a stranger with no heaven above her / Keeping in motion because fear is an ocean / nursing the pain that flows in my veins / It pierces my heart with soul-rending sorrow / the history we're writing has no tomorrow

—Chris D., "Black Temptation"
from The Flesh Eaters album *I Used to Be Pretty*, 2019

I grew up in Riverside, California, in a conservative Catholic family. Despite my mother's religious worldview, she loved movies. On most afternoons in the early 1960s she'd set up her ironing board in the den, progeny staked out cross-legged on the floor, watching films from the past thirty years. There were early-morning movies, late-morning movies, all-afternoon movies, prime-time movies, and all-night movies on Los Angeles's TV stations. Movies—albeit in mediocre prints interrupted by car dealers' commercials—gushed forth like a wildcat driller's oil strike. Picking up *TV Guide* was like rolling the dice, or spinning the roulette wheel.

One of the earliest crime films I remember was *Car 99* (1935) with Fred MacMurray and Ann Sheridan. Not noir by a longshot, but an old-fashioned action picture with an intrepid prowl-car cop up against racketeers. Lots of Bogart as well, not just classics such as *High Sierra*, *The Maltese Falcon*, and *The Big Sleep*, but *Angels with Dirty Faces*, *The Roaring Twenties*, *The Petrified Forest*, and *Dead End*. Cary Grant in *Big Brown Eyes*. James Cagney in *The Public Enemy*, *Lady Killer*, and *White Heat*. The Thin Man series with William Powell and Myrna Loy.

Then there were the sci-fi-noir masterpieces that combined excellent performances with breakneck mise-en-scène, frighteningly realistic effects, and a creepy, pitch-black ambience, among them *Invasion of the Body Snatchers*, *It! The Terror from Beyond Space*, and Paul Landres's all-but-forgotten Southern California gothic *The Vampire*, with John Beal and Coleen Gray—films that gave me my most vividly remembered nightmares.

I enrolled in an all-boys parochial high school with no preconceived notions about the world. My teen crushes were not inordinately demoralizing—until those cheerleaders made fun of me. Not only because my flirtations were clumsy, but because my mom was the secretary at their all-girls school.

I'd drive over there with my younger brother every afternoon to pick up my mom, which gave me time to hang around the uniformed gals waiting for rides. Nothing but cold shoulders from the jock-obsessed cheerleaders, so my attention drifted to the big-haired, lipsticked "bad girls," sent to St. Francis to have their drug problems and/or sexual peccadillos straightened out. They were fun and non-judgmental, and their bratty audacity had allure. I idolized them. They would often materialize in the songs and prose I'd write in the years to come.

Another formative incident: a teacher admonished a bunch of us for getting too rambunctious in class. But only Ernie, the lone Black student, was singled out for a trip to the principal. I loudly demanded to know why. Steam billowing from his ears, the teacher sent me into exile with Ernie. That teacher may not have been a racist, but with the jocks there was no doubt. They were mean, racist, sexist, and given to ganging up on weird artistic guys, nonwhite guys, possibly gay guys. My enduring hatred for sports stemmed from constant contact with these sociopaths.[1] One of many factors that cultivated a rebellious, misanthropic punk.

By now TV was also offering a bonanza of European art films, often subtitled, airing Saturday nights on channel 9. The UK's gritty, angry young man films held special interest, blending alienated characters—who would now be seen as "punk"—with stories dark as any noir: *Look Back in Anger*, *The Loneliness of the Long Distance Runner*, *Saturday Night and Sunday Morning*, *Billy Liar*, *The Servant*, and especially *This Sporting Life* had considerable impact.

I schemed detours around my mother's roadblocks to acclaimed but controversial films (many X-rated) showing in theaters. Fortunately, my English teacher—a hep priest—intervened, assuring my mother I was mature enough. Suddenly I was taking in neo-noirs such as *Bullitt*, *Point Blank*, and *Pretty Poison*, and more controversial films like *Easy Rider*, *Midnight Cowboy*, *Rosemary's Baby*, *Belle de Jour*, *End of the Road*, *Accident*, and *Last Summer*.

Before I left for college in 1970, I could distinguish between regular crime films and film noir. I saw *Criss Cross*, *On the Waterfront*, *Angel Face*, *The Lady from Shanghai*, *Touch of Evil*, *Kansas City Confidential*, *The Killing* ... too many to count. I even organized campus screenings of *Out of the Past*, *Raw Deal*, *They Live by Night*, and *99 River Street*.

The most influential proto-punk film (shot in 1969 but not released until late 1970 due to Warner Bros.' bewilderment) was the psychedelic gangster movie *Performance*, directed by Donald Cammell and Nicolas Roeg. Mick Jagger is a reclusive rock star who has lost his creative "demon" and James Fox is the sadistic, repressed, on-the-run mobster who finds refuge in the rocker's decrepit mansion. The mash-up of visual styles is mesmerizing. When Jagger's playful, astute muse (Anita Pallenberg) explains to an ultra-high Fox—in bed—that his problems stem from an unwillingness to accept the female side of his persona, Fox has a psychotic break(through). 'Shroomed to the gills, he hallucinates Jagger as his gang-boss, performing the William Burroughs–influenced "Memo from Turner."

Here's the logical place to suggest that The Rolling Stones were an essential progenitor of punk rock, paving the way for a movement that began with UK bands The Sex Pistols, The Clash, The Damned, The Vibrators, X-Ray Spex, and Siouxsie and the Banshees, all circa 1975. From their very first albums, the Stones reconfigured Black American R&B and white pop; their songs scandalized the pop music industry and broke down walls for the acceptability of dark subject matter in the Top 40.

> I was born in a crossfire hurricane / And I howled at my ma in the driving rain / I was raised by a toothless, bearded hag / I was schooled with a strap right across my back / I was drowned, I was washed up and left for dead / I was crowned with a spike right thru my head
> —The Rolling Stones, "Jumpin' Jack Flash"
> #1 single in America, April 1968

The Doors followed suit in California with dark hits like "Break on Through," "Light My Fire," and

---

[1] It's obvious to me now that not all athletes are cut from the same cloth, and many are diametrically opposed to this stereotype.

Vice. And Versa.

Mick Jagger. And Mick Jagger.

James Fox. And James Fox.

See them all in a film about fantasy. And reality. Vice. And versa.

performance.

James Fox/Mick Jagger/Anita Pallenberg/Michele Breton

Written by Donald Cammell/Directed by Donald Cammell & Nicolas Roeg/Produced by Sanford Lieberson in Technicolor. A Goodtimes Enterprises Production from Warner Bros. THIS FILM IS RATED (X) NO ONE UNDER 17 ADMITTED
Hear Mick Jagger sing "Memo From Turner" in the original sound track album on Warner Bros. Records and tapes.

"People Are Strange." In New York, The Velvet Underground, with the blessing of their discoverer/benefactor Andy Warhol, released previously unimaginable pop songs such as "I'm Waiting for the Man," "Femme Fatale," "Venus in Furs," "Heroin," "White Light/White Heat," and "Sister Ray."

It's impossible to imagine the next wave of ear-blasting, anarchic garage rockers—The Sonics, The MC5, The Stooges (fronted by wild boy Iggy Pop), and eventually The Ramones, without their spiritual big brothers—Mick Jagger, Jim Morrison, and Lou Reed—coming before them.

Suddenly there was a school of rock that chronicled dark, taboo subject matter: addiction, prostitution, polysexuality, sadomasochism, crime, political revolt, suicide, and murder. These artists were not rock 'n' roll heroes—they were the antiheroes of an edgy, scary new breed of pop. As 1960s Los Angeles garage-rockers The Standells famously sang, "Sometimes Good Guys Don't Wear White." A sentiment apropos to the birth of punk as much as it was an earlier era of film noir.

That spirit of rebellion became so radically revamped by the UK and New York punk explosions of late 1975, and the Los Angeles, San Francisco, and Melbourne booms of late 1976, that it became quite clear to me—a wannabe rocker who always felt musically unqualified—that "Hey, these guys couldn't sing or play their instruments at first either!" My first wife, Bonnie, and I had just put out our own poetry anthology, *Bongo Chalice*—why not do it with music, too? Poet Patti Smith had done that very thing in 1975 in New York. The do-it-yourself ethos became a creed many of my musician friends lived by in the late 1970s, and that has continued, off and on, to this day. We felt a kinship with the British and French New Waves in cinema—a forceful, unconscious solidarity. And before that, of course, there was film noir.

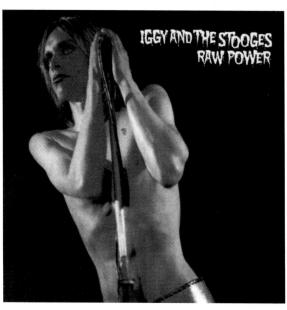

I'm the runaway son of the nuclear A bomb / a streetwalking cheetah with a hotfoot of napalm / I am the world's forgotten boy / the one who searches to destroy

—Iggy Pop, "Search and Destroy"
from The Stooges album *Raw Power*, 1973

This proto-punk piledriver could be the theme song of Sam Wild, the loose cannon sociopath played by Lawrence Tierney in director Robert Wise's 1947 noir, *Born to Kill*. There is more than a bit of ironic self-reflection in Iggy's words, however, whereas Tierney's blast-furnace paranoiac reflects on nothing but the outsized chip on his shoulder, his resentful sense of entitlement to "get what's mine"—money, power, adulation, and a ruthless woman who has a similar bottomless hole of *want* where her conscience should be.

My brother, he was a stranger man / and I asked him for release / he said it wouldn't do me no good / and he sent for the police / well, they busted me for nothing / because they said I was insane / they've already let my body go / but they've locked away my brain

—Ian Hunter, "The Moon Upstairs"
from the Mott the Hoople album *Brain Capers*,
1971 (dedicated to the memory of James Dean)

Mental health issues—real or engineered by shadowy Machiavellian family or institutional figures—not only crop up in many noirs but in lots of rock 'n' roll as it mutated into punk. Noir classics such as *Spellbound*, *My Name Is Julia Ross*, *Gaslight*, *Experiment Perilous*, *The Dark Mirror*, *Beware My Lovely*, *The Hidden Room*, *High Wall*, *Shock Corridor*, et al. would fill pages with titles. This subgenre has remained prevalent not only in punk songwriting, but also in numerous neo-noirs, from *After Dark, My Sweet* (1990) through *Shutter Island* (2010) to *Unsane* (2018).

One aspect of the punk ethos that outsiders didn't understand—and still don't—is the uncompromising emotional commitment to following a moral compass, the desire to tell the truth and not allow big business or politics to hijack someone's personal struggle or self-image for their own cold-blooded agendas. Punks were not interested in following the clarion call of selfish individualism. We believed in doing what's right, even if no one else is watching and your motivations might be misconstrued and your safety jeopardized.

Of course, the noir element in both punk and film (as in real life) can manifest in characters *not* realizing how important it is to adhere to their moral compass; some may not recognize it until it's too late, or—worst of all—they never realize it at all, with fatal results.

In every street and every station / Kids fight like different nations / And it's brawn against brain / And it's knife against chain / But it's all young blood / Flowing down the drain
—Joe Strummer, "Last Gang in Town" from The Clash album *Give 'Em Enough Rope*, 1978

Not all juvenile delinquency opuses are noir, but it's a subgenre that noticeably appears in punk music. Many borderline noirs, especially from the 1950s, exploited the middle class's concern over teen crime, drug use, and promiscuity. Nicholas Ray's classic *Rebel Without a Cause* (1955), plus his 1948 debut *They Live by Night* (as well as 1949's somewhat disappointing *Knock on Any Door*) cover a range of JD tropes as young people struggle to reach adulthood in an unwelcoming world.

Other examples proliferated in the fifties: *Crime in the Streets*; *Blackboard Jungle*; Roger Corman's ultra-low-budget drive-in sagas *Teenage Doll* and *Sorority Girl*; Robert Altman's *The Delinquents*; and *Teenage Crime Wave*. Perhaps even more entertaining are the sleaze-noir JD films of the early 1960s like *Look in Any Window* (with Paul Anka and Ruth Roman!), Alexander Singer's *A Cold Wind in August*, and the disturbing *Who Killed Teddy Bear?* with warped teen Sal Mineo stalking Juliet Prowse.

Then there are the amour fou noirs—narratives with many musical counterparts, not only in punk but also other pop music subgenres, from goth to country. In fact, country/folk music may be the oldest manifestation of noir in popular culture, their progenitors the regional, folk murder ballads of the nineteenth century.

By late 1983, I was sick of the "louder, faster, shorter" trend in punk. I disbanded the existing lineup of my band The Flesh Eaters, looking toward a more melodic, acoustic-infused approach. A similar thing was happening among musician friends. John Doe, Exene Cervenka, and DJ Bonebrake of X joined Blaster Dave Alvin to form a non-amplified country side-group, The Knitters. I was hanging out with Jeffrey Lee Pierce of The Gun Club and Dan Stuart of Green on Red, both of whom were big country/blues fans. Chip and Tony Kinman, of the politically hardcore punk combo The Dils, switched styles, forming the dark, offbeat country punk band Rank and File.[2] Aussie Nick Cave left the dynamically dissonant The Birthday Party to form The Bad Seeds. With influences ranging from Leonard Cohen to folk murder ballads to Protestant mysticism, Cave continues with various Bad Seeds lineups to this day.

None of these people were copying each other. It was an explosion of unconscious synchronicity. I had met kindred spirit Julie Christensen (who would sing backup with Leonard Cohen in the early '90s) while producing a song for Top Jimmy, a cover of Faron Young's "Hello, Walls." She joined me singing backup as well as occasional co-lead vocals on *Time Stands Still*, the de facto debut of the Divine Horsemen (released in 1984 under the name Chris D./Divine Horsemen). Prior to creating that album, I discovered a volume called *American Murder Ballads*, a collection of nineteenth century lyrics from frontier songs, chronicles of tragic, doomed romance. Not only did it coincide with my worldview, it served as evidence of a link between European literary Romanticism and nineteenth-century American pop culture. It was a sturdy foundation when formulating ideas for the first Divine Horsemen album. Amour fou noir, especially titles such as *Angel Face*, *Out of the Past*, *Criss Cross*, *Raw Deal*, *They Live by Night*, *In a Lonely Place*, *Shockproof*, *On Dangerous Ground*, Joseph Losey's *The Prowler* and *The Sleeping Tiger*, *Pépé le Moko*, *La bête humaine* (and scores of other French noirs starring Jean Gabin) have been—and still are—a huge influence on my songwriting and crime fiction.

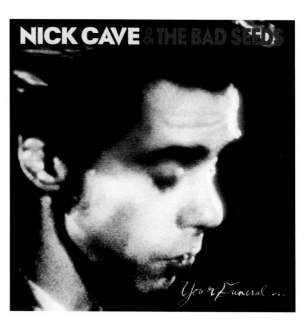

These lyrics by Nick Cave come from an album permeated with amour fou and give off a distinctly unhealthy *Night of the Hunter* vibe.

Here I am, little lamb / Let all the bells in whoredom ring / All the crooked bitches that she was / (Mongers of pain) / Saw the moon / Become a fang / Your funeral, my trial
—Nick Cave, "Your Funeral, My Trial"
from the album of the same name, 1986

Literary influences, from hardboiled crime to the Beat Generation to more traditional writers, inspired many punk songwriters I know. Romantic poets and French symbolists from nineteenth-century Europe often plunged into stygian depths of despair and transcendence, inspiring artists like Jim Morrison and Patti Smith. They passed the torch to equally inspirational transgressive Surrealists and Dada practitioners of the early twentieth century. Even more traditional writers like Faulkner, Hemingway, Fitzgerald, and Steinbeck were well-known to my colleagues in punk.

I'd already read most of Chandler, Hammett, and James M. Cain by the time I hit college. By the late 1970s, I'd discovered Jim Thompson, David Goodis, Horace McCoy, W. R. Burnett, Georges Simenon, William Lindsay Gresham, and lesser but still good writers such as Charles Willeford, Harry Whittington, Charles Williams, and Day Keene. In the early 2000s I made the acquaintance of sleaze-pulp lost souls Gil Brewer and Orrie Hitt, a pair of loser noir/sex pulp-meisters.

Of course, the controversial, unclassifiable giant William Burroughs, who came up with the Beats, heav-

---

2 Several Rank and File songs appear on the soundtrack to the 1985 neo-noir *To Live and Die in LA*.

ily influenced everyone from David Bowie to Patti Smith to Lou Reed to David Cronenberg. Along with Chandler, Hammett, Cain, and Jim Thompson, Burroughs (and streetwise writers such as Charles Bukowski and John Rechy) inspired compatriots John Doe and Exene of X, Jeffrey Lee Pierce of The Gun Club, Lydia Lunch, rock scribe Byron Coley, and myself.

> I should've stayed home on my ladder to fire / made good, good friends, the devil in the flesh / dig that crazy grave and find a victim / and kill the killer inside my heart / smile at me and make love to the ramrod / who's riding herd inside my head
> —Chris D., "Kiss Tomorrow Goodbye"
> from the Divine Horsemen album *Snake Handler*, 1987

In fact, there are two songs on that album where I took numerous titles from existential and hardboiled books and movies and mashed them up William Burroughs/Brion Gysin–style to form lyrics. "Kiss Tomorrow Goodbye" is, of course, from the Horace McCoy novel, as is the phrase "I Should've Stayed Home" (another McCoy title); "Ladder to Fire" (a symbolist erotic volume by Anaïs Nin); "The Devil in the Flesh" (amour fou by Raymond Radiguet); "Dig That Crazy Grave" (trashy Shell Scott novel by Richard Prather); "Find a Victim" (detective novel by Ross Macdonald); and "the killer inside my heart" (homage to Thompson's "The Killer Inside Me"). "Ramrod" (from the 1947 noir western) has among many other references in the second and third verses, "The Naked Kiss" (Sam Fuller's 1964 neo-noir) and "Play It as It Lays," the novel by Joan Didion.

Punk is not about the over-the-top images on which exploitative media has always concentrated, those superficial aspects of punk's most extreme visual signifiers, i.e., the Mohawks, studded collars and wristbands, combat boots, makeshift safety pin jewelry, provocative piercings. My fashion and grooming tastes hewed closer to *Rebel Without a Cause*–era James Dean, *Purple Noon*–era Alain Delon, or even *Bullitt*-era Steve McQueen than the outrageous looks of The Sex Pistols' Johnny "Rotten" Lydon, The Damned, or UK bands like GBH and The Exploited, whose visual tropes garnered more attention than their music.

Likewise, punk's spirit was often distorted like some broken funhouse mirror, not only by the sensation-hungry news media but by the grievance-fueled music and lifestyle of the second punk wave of the early 1980s, the smash-everything-whether-it's-good-or-bad gangs of hardcore, skinhead hooligans speed-riffing and thrashing their way into dumpster-fire oblivion on both sides of the Atlantic.

Punk musicians—usually singer/songwriters—have also manifested noir in other media, especially motion pictures. In 1984, Italian director Roberto Faenza cast John "Rotten" Lydon in the underrated neo-noir *Corrupt* (aka *Order of Death* aka *Cop Killer*). Harvey Keitel and Sylvia Sidney (as Lydon's grandmother!) costarred. Ennio Morricone contributed a pulsating score. The Clash's Joe Strummer appeared in Alex Cox's *Straight to Hell* (1987), Jim Jarmusch's *Mystery Train* (1989), and Aki Kaurismäki's *I Hired a Contract Killer* (1990). Lee Ving from the band Fear assayed supporting roles in many films, including *Flashdance* (1983), *Black Moon Rising* (1986), and *The Taking of Beverly Hills* (1991).

Black Flag's Henry Rollins had supporting roles in Michael Mann's epic *Heat* (1995) and David Lynch's superior neo-noir nightmare *Lost Highway* (1997). Nick Cave cavorts in John Hillcoat's ragged but energetic Australian prison saga, *Ghosts of the Civil Dead* (1988), which he cowrote. He also wrote the screenplays for the excellent revisionist Aussie western *The Proposition* (2005) and the rollicking Cajun crime film *Lawless* (2012), starring Tom Hardy and Guy Pearce, both also helmed by Hillcoat. Lydia Lunch has appeared in countless fiction and nonfiction movies, her most visible being the erotic suspenser *Kiss Napoleon Goodbye* (1990), costarring Rollins and Beth B.

X's John Doe and I, along with Dave Alvin (then guitarist/songwriter for The Blasters), made our collective movie debuts in *Border Radio* (1987), directed by Allison Anders, Kurt Voss, and Dean Lent. My character's name, Jeff Bailey, was an homage to Mitchum's doomed ex-detective in *Out of the Past*. *Border Radio*, which began shooting in 1985, originated as a neo-noir, with fugitive rock musician Jeff, along with his estranged wife, Luanna (Luanna Anders), stalked by seemingly good-natured roadie Chris (Chris

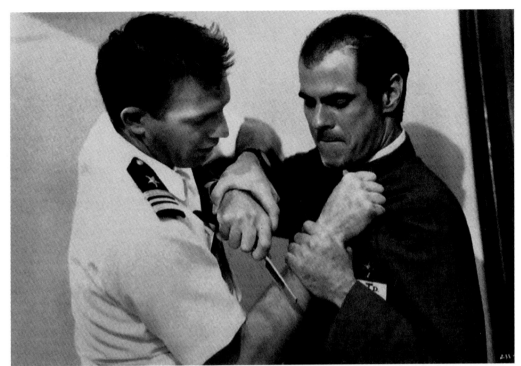

Kevin Costner trying not to get slashed by assassin Chris D. in director Roger Donaldson's *No Way Out*, a loose remake of *The Big Clock*.

Shearer), who turns out to be homicidal. When funds ran low, forcing a six-month shooting hiatus, the filmmakers reworked the script into a quirky comedy drama (à la early Jim Jarmusch), and Chris's roadie ended up just another deluded, egocentric loser, alongside the musician characters played by me and John.

I also had a role in *No Way Out* (1987), Roger Donaldson's extremely loose remake of *The Big Clock* (1948). Original villain Charles Laughton's hitman bodyguard (played by Harry Morgan) was split into a pair of government contras played by me and Marshall Bell, doing the bidding of a fixer (Will Patton) working for the Secretary of Defense (Gene Hackman). After Hackman accidentally kills his mistress (Sean Young), Patton—with the aid of these two homicidal henchmen—hangs the crime on a patsy, a naval officer (Kevin Costner) who'd been romancing Young. Right now, John Doe is starring as Frank Bigelow in a remake of the classic *DOA*, currently in postproduction. I have a vivid memory of seeing Nicholas Ray's *In a Lonely Place* with John (it's one of his favorite movies) in 1978 at the Encore, a long-gone Hollywood revival theater. As John recently mentioned to me, comparing film noir to his arrival in Los Angeles back in the day, "It's where the action is." ■

PROFILES
SECTION TWO

RELUCTANT HERO
THE RESTLESS CHARM OF WILLIAM HOLDEN

By Rachel Walther

William Holden is not an actor synonymous with film noir. More often, his name conjures the image of a mid-century adventurer, serving his country bravely in World War II or Korea in between romancing Grace Kelly or Sophia Loren. But throughout his career, the actor best known for sitting on champagne glasses and blowing up a bridge in Thailand brought an ambivalence and a brooding restlessness to his characters that distanced them from the mainstream—and sometimes thrust them into the realm of darkness we hold so dear.

Holden's early films generally featured him as a pretty young man opposite older female leads—he earned Barbara Stanwyck's love in his debut feature *Golden Boy* (1939), courted Jean Arthur on the frontier in *Arizona* (1940), and made Frances Dee a home in the newlywed comedy *Meet the Stewarts* (1942). After a wartime stint as a first lieutenant in the Air Force's First Motion Picture Unit, the actor's postwar years at Paramount and Columbia were of leading-man stature but uneven quality.

Holden's first foray into the shadows came in *The Dark Past* (1948). Director Rudolph Maté's investigation into the subconscious features Holden as escaped convict Al Walker, who holes up with his gang at the country house of criminal psychologist Andrew Collins (Lee J. Cobb). Collins remains calm even as Walker's gang menaces his guests at gunpoint, and over the course of the evening the doctor delves into Walker's past to unearth the root of his criminality. Holden appears out of his depth and wholly uncomfortable, with hair and wardrobe seemingly borrowed directly from *High Sierra* along with a Duke Mantee swagger that doesn't match his flinty midwestern twang. But as the film progresses, Holden's naivete, so incongruous with the tough-guy persona he's flaunting, becomes the key to uncovering childhood memories he's tried to bury through a life of crime. When Collins probes Walker's default violence by asking, "Do you think pulling that trigger will stop your nightmares?" he forces the fugitive to face an enemy more powerful than any rival gang or prison warden: his own mind.

The Dark Past was a remake of Columbia's *Blind Alley* (1939), directed by Charles Vidor. The original adaptation of James Warwick's play has a flat B-movie tenor, with Chester Morris in Holden's role and Ralph Bellamy sized for Cobb's tweed jacket. Morris portrays the troubled fugitive as more ruthless, a man with a weathered stare outrunning ghosts rather than a tough boy outrunning himself. In the end, Morris's hoodlum is dealt with in the Production Code's preferred manner for

Al Walker (Holden) reluctantly allows himself to be examined Dr. Andrew Collins (Lee J. Cobb) in *The Dark Past.*

dispatching criminals; by 1949, Holden's Walker is allowed to face a new day, a broken man too far gone for literal rehabilitation but now armed with the tools to live the rest of his life behind bars with a modicum of self-awareness. Morris's ignorant snarl and pugnacious mug may have been more apt casting, but it's Holden's frantic vulnerability and Maté's tense pacing that yields the more enduring version of Warwick's story.

Throughout the remainder of the 1940s Holden appeared in some decent Westerns and bubbly comedies, often billed below a more prominent female star. He's the kindhearted farmer opposite Loretta Young's soulful pioneer woman in *Rachel and the Stranger* (1948), the earnest ex-GI husband to Jeanne Crain's expectant mother in *Apartment for Peggy* (1948), and the con man foiled by Lucille Ball's featherbrained secretary in *Miss Grant Takes Richmond* (1949). In 1950 Holden was beginning his second decade in the business and, as costar Nancy Olson reflected in an interview, in "a ragged part of his career." Billy Wilder's *Sunset Boulevard* was about to shoot when Montgomery Clift, originally slated for the role of Joe Gillis, backed out at the last minute. Holden was hastily chosen as a replacement with Wilder's wary approval, and the actor imbued Joe with a decade of stored-up depth that there had been little call for in his previous features.

Holden plays screenwriter Joe not as a tough, seen-it-all Hollywood veteran but as a normal guy in his early thirties, playacting roles he's seen on screen. When a couple of creditors bust into his room demanding payment, he's Sam Spade sarcastically confronting Lieutenant Dundy and Detective Polhaus; with Norma Desmond (Gloria Swanson) he tries coming across as a big shot, but when she sees through his act (and the holes in his checkbook) he becomes a sulky teenager with folded arms; with

Dead Man's Float: Holden gets fished out of Gloria Swanson's pool "like a harpooned baby whale" in *Sunset Boulevard*.

aspiring writer Betty Schaefer (Olson) he's breezy and charming, generous with advice and confident in himself.

Joe's postmortem narration aims to maintain the facade of a man in control, but it doesn't always match up with what's on screen. His drowned voice-over won't acknowledge any sincerity in his relationship with Norma—it was all a transaction gone wrong—but in their scenes Holden's face conveys a host of emotions: guilt, pity, tenderness. His cynicism, though delightful, is a retreat into self-preservation. Joe is willing to own up to mistakes made in pursuit of his own needs, but reluctant to admit those forged out of compassion or affection toward Norma. His decision to stay with her after their screenplay is finished is partly to avoid the stresses of the back rent on his one-room apartment and overdue car payments, but also out of fear of the past. Since he arrived in Hollywood, Joe's been leery of "that $35 a week job at the copy desk at the *Dayton Evening Post*," a fate that he views as the end of everything. It's the fear of that workaday hell that encourages him to exploit Norma and also to collaborate with Betty, paving the way for a brighter future while simultaneously digging his own grave.

Sunset Boulevard earned Holden an Academy Award nomination for Best Actor. Its success catapulted him to the A-list. His follow-up film was *Union Station* (1950), a police procedural baked in the *Naked City* mold of on-location photography and just-the-facts delivery. The plot is the real star of the show, a recounting of the efforts to find a ruthless kidnapper who has absconded with a millionaire's blind daughter and murders everyone who comes between him and the ransom. Holden's Lieutenant William Cochrane doesn't have much to do besides deliver his lines while looking stern

and commanding. Still channeling Bogart when talking with Joyce (Nancy Olson again), the good-natured secretary who sets the investigation in motion, he delivers a line straight out of *Casablanca*: "When anyone asks me to stick my neck out, I want to know who's doing the asking." But Holden's hard-nosed scenes are sweetened by a series of charming boy-meets-girl exchanges with Olson and the scene-stealing faffing of old-school Irish detective Inspector Donnelly (played by *The Naked City*'s Barry Fitzgerald). Joyce chides Cochrane throughout the film for his unnecessary gruffness, the issue becoming a source of laughter between them. Cochrane isn't all bark, and eventually risks his life to save the kidnapped girl. With director Maté again at the helm, the film concludes with an unforgettable dreamscape chase through the subterranean rail networks of central Los Angeles.

In 1952, Holden played another scribe in director William Dieterle's *The Turning Point*. Based on a story by Horace McCoy, the film depicts a corruption scandal in a midwestern city that rips through the local government and into the police department. John Conroy (Edmond O'Brien) is the newly appointed special prosecutor charged with cleaning up the mess, and Mandy Waycross (Alexis Smith) is his gal Friday. Jerry McKibbon (Holden) is a local reporter and fly in the ointment, an old friend of John's who is dubious that the investigation will dig up anything beyond a few sacrificial lambs cut loose by the powers that be. In contrast to O'Brien's wide emotional landscape, from conducting interrogations with a staccato, earnest tone to speaking softly and warmly when addressing Smith, Holden's reporter remains stoic and aloof, saying whatever's on his mind—even if it's unpopular—with assurance and an air of preoccupation. Mandy is initially repulsed by Jerry's implacability, dispensing a verdict that could be leveled against many Holden characters: "The detached cynical observer faintly amused by the follies of other humans." But Jerry and Mandy inevitably end their confrontations in a clinch, cutting out would-be suitor John.

During his own investigation, Jerry discovers that John's father, Matt (Tom Tully), a local police inspector, is on the payroll of syndicate boss Neil Eichelberger (Ed Begley). Unwilling to shatter John's illusions about his father's integrity, Jerry tells Matt he'll keep silent if the inspector withdraws from his crooked sideline, an ultimatum that produces fatal results. It's a testament to Holden's appeal that halfway through the film Jerry

The relationship between Joe (Holden) and Norma (Gloria Swanson) is more complex than his voice-over would have us believe.

Reporter William Holden wields both pen and pistol in *The Turning Point*.

has stolen John's girl and instigated the death of John's father, all while continuing to denigrate his best friend's investigative efforts, and we're still rooting for him over O'Brien's stalwart prosecutor. Eventually the men put aside their personal beefs to work together, finding a key witness who breaks the case wide open. The movie's title could be referring to a few things: the apartment building fire ordered by Eichelberger, which claims many lives and galvanizes John into ratcheting up his investigation, or the moment when Jerry finally drops his hard-edged objectivity and becomes one of Mandy's "human follies," consigning himself to the greater good by making the ultimate sacrifice. In many of Holden's films, his cynical men move through life as if sleepwalking, only awakening when they examine themselves fully and discover previously unarticulated truths, love, or patriotism that drives them to their destiny.

Holden's next project reteamed him with creative good-luck charm Billy Wilder. The resulting film, *Stalag 17* (1953), garnered a Best Actor win for Holden and a Best Director nomination for Wilder at the Oscars that year. Holden plays Sergeant J.J. Sefton, a shady wheeler-dealer POW who trades in contraband goods and brews homemade hooch. Happy to profit off his fellow GIs and Nazi guards alike, Sefton would be right at home as roommate to Richard Widmark's Skip in *Pickup on South Street*. Holden plays Sefton smoothly and deliberately, an unshaven panther possessively prowling around the barracks. When Sefton is suspected to be the mole funneling intel to the Nazis,

Holden won the 1954 Academy Award for Best Actor playing wheeler-dealer POW J.J. Sefton in *Stalag 17*.

it's up to the blackguard himself to ferret out the real rat and save his own skin. Despite being unfairly viewed as the lowest of the low by his fellow GIs, Holden never allows Sefton to display frustration when he's being scrutinized and accused, only registering moments of sadness or confusion when he's alone with his thoughts.

In his war films Holden's characters may behave valiantly by the closing credits, but those acts are often the result of blackmail, coercion, or sheer terror. In *The Counterfeit Traitor* (1962), Holden plays Swedish oil trader Eric Erickson, who willingly applies his country's neutrality toward his own politics at the outbreak of World War II. But after a visit from British intelligence, he learns that his company will be blacklisted by the Allies unless he engages in espionage against the Nazis. Holden shuns any display of heroism or integrity in Erickson's behavior, allowing the oil trader to show nothing but self-pity and resentment about his mission until he becomes thoroughly shaken by the brutal policies of the Third Reich. He converts to the Allies' cause after witnessing the selfless heroism of his compatriot Marianne Möllendorf (Lilli Palmer).

At the midway point of *The Bridge on the River Kwai* (1957), Holden's soldier Shears is breezily satisfied after escaping from Japanese Colonel Saito's prison camp. When he's asked by British Major Warden (Jack Hawkins) to return to the jungle in order to pinpoint the location of the camp and destroy it, Shears becomes gasping and fearful, admitting that he's just an "ordinary swab jockey second class" who impersonated a lieutenant in the hopes of getting better treatment as a POW. Only after Warden gives him the option of returning home in handcuffs for his deception does Shears resign himself to the noble deed: "As long as I'm hooked, I might as well volunteer." Even Sefton's eventual heroism in *Stalag 17* comes as much from a selfish wish to escape the POW camp as an altruistic one to ferry a fellow GI to safety. He cracks wise to the very end: "I told you guys I'm no escape artist, but for the first time I like the odds."

The Key (1958) finds him back in the European theater as Captain David Ross, commanding a fleet of doomed tugboats in the Atlantic for the Canadian Army in mid-1941. Ross isn't a scheming "out for number one" Sefton, but a normal Joe Gillis type anxiously playacting the role of war hero out of genuine concern for his men—and himself. Ross's outfit is tasked with rescuing Allied ships damaged by U-boats and Nazi aircraft, and the casualties are running at nearly 100 percent. He becomes so inured to the dire straits of the Canadian and British forces that when he receives a call telling him that the United States has just entered the war, he snaps back, "Oh yeah? What side?" Holden's Ross is a reluctant hero, a man dragging himself through one dangerous mission after another because he has nowhere else to run. The past of peacetime is long gone, and there's no future on the horizon.

Holden also displayed a cynical edge in many of his on-screen romances, appearing uncomfortable at the idea of committing even to a one-night stand. He initially shrugs off advances by Nancy Kwan's working girl in *The World of Suzie Wong* (1960) ("I like, but can't afford") and Kay Lenz's free-spirited hippie in *Breezy* (1973) ("All we add up to is a dirty joke") in an effort to stay independent and unencumbered. He accepts Faye Dunaway's dinner invitation in *Network* (1976) with the playful caveat, "I've got to warn you, I don't do anything on my first date." By playing hard to get in a manner usually reserved for mid-century women, Holden retains his aura as mysterious loner; as a result, every smile or scrap of affection from him becomes a major win.

The turning points for Holden's everymen come in many forms, but there's always an evolution or a shock that changes his character irrevocably. Eddie Muller has often noted that Holden would have been the perfect Philip Marlowe, but Marlowe's unshakably cynical core and resignation in the face of the world's treacheries reflect an inner resolve that Holden's characters are still in the process of discovering. It's that vulnerability and moodiness—with a side of wiseacre—that makes William Holden right at home in Noir City, even when the forecast calls for full Technicolor. ■

STANLEY BAKER

LOVING A THIEVING BOY

RAY BANKS

"The most striking thing about Stanley Baker when he walks into a restaurant is how extraordinarily like a gangster he looks," wrote Susan Barnes in her 1964 profile for the *Sunday Express*. An easy refrain, oft repeated throughout his career, but Stanley Baker was more than the sum of his parts. A gifted stage actor and alumnus of the Birmingham Rep (alongside such luminaries as Laurence Olivier and John Gielgud), Baker bought himself out of his Rank contract and would have a short but illustrious career as a producer-star of *Zulu* (1964) and *Robbery* (1967), as well as uncredited producer on *The Italian Job* (1969). His screen performances provided the bridge between the gentlemanly stars of the postwar era, typified by Kenneth More and Jack Hawkins, to the working-class heroes of Albert Finney and Michael Caine. Before Baker, working-class characters tended to provide either comic relief or salt-of-the-earth sentiment, designed to bolster the middle- and upper-class stars, who represented moral strength and aspirational patriotism. As such, a rising star with a regional accent was treated with some suspicion by the studio establishment. Baker's breakthrough role as the bullying fraud Bennett in *The Cruel Sea* (1953) would typecast him as a heavy for the majority of his early career, along with roles as the murderous Erik Bland in *Hell Below Zero* (1954) and Mordred in *Knights of the Round Table* (1954).

"FOUR MEN. EACH FROM A DIFFERENT WALK OF LIFE..."

The heavy takes on shades of heroism in *The Good Die Young* (1954), in which Baker plays Mike Morgan, a former prizefighter turned armed robber, who is introduced pre-heist alongside his three fellow thieves. All four men have woman and money troubles: Mike lost his hand after an ill-advised final bout and his life savings to his ne'er-do-well brother-in-law thanks to a moment of weakness on his wife's part; former clerk Joe (Richard Basehart) is trying to rescue his pregnant wife (Joan Collins) from the clutches of her oppressively clingy mother; Eddie (John Ireland) is a cuckolded war hero, whose bit-player wife (Gloria Grahame) is stepping out on him; and Rave (Laurence Harvey) is a psychopathic rake, whose moneyed better half has called time on his parasitic, philandering behavior and is about to cut him off. All have seen active service, some distinguished (or apparently so—Rave's decoration at El Alamein was thanks to his murder of six unconscious Germans), and all have returned to Civvy Street in a state of moral poverty. They are easy pickings for the manipulative Rave, who has a plan to rob a hundred grand in used banknotes. As plans go, it is less a meticulous heist than it is an impulsive one (though Rave has a stolen getaway car and firearms to hand), and as such it is doomed to failure, with each of the robbers meeting his maker by bullet or, in one particularly nasty case, a passing train.

Mike is the most sympathetically drawn of the quartet, his ambitions modest and his misfortunes great. His Dutch-angled breakdown is presented as a keenly felt moment of despair: "Stone deaf in one ear, half blind and only one hand! What sort of man does that make me?" And Mike is the sole robber to turn his back on the job for moral reasons, only to leave it open to one of Rave's bullets. He ends his life as tragic antihero, his head in a puddle and the sound of a referee counting him out for good. While the other robbers have their own memorable deaths, it is Mike's that resonates the most.

Rave (Laurence Harvey, second from right) suckers Mike (Baker), Eddie (John Ireland), and Joe (Richard Basehart) into a suicide heist.

Bannion returns to Wandsworth Prison under the watchful eye of Barrows (Patrick Magee).

"ALL MY SADNESS, ALL MY JOY, COME FROM LOVING A THIEVING BOY..."

Baker would play a more morally ambivalent antihero in Joseph Losey's *The Criminal* (aka *The Concrete Jungle*, 1960). Jimmy Sangster's original story was passed to Baker by Hammer head Michael Carreras for consideration, but Losey was not a fan, later pronouncing it "a direct plagiarism from practically every American prison film that had ever been made" and enlisting Liverpool playwright Alun Owen to give the story some verisimilitude. But any viewer expecting realism from a Losey film is likely to be disappointed.

Baker plays Johnny Bannion (apparently based partly on flamboyant Soho enforcer Albert "Italian Al" Dimes), a gruff professional thief whose release from prison affords him the opportunity to relieve a racetrack of forty grand. The heist itself is almost perversely straightforward—and so inconsequential it happens offscreen—but Bannion struggles to hold on to his ill-gotten gains. No sooner has he pulled off the heist than he's back inside, bartering his loot for freedom and running afoul of former accomplices. While Bannion may exude the air of top dog—the kind of man who can make a former flame demented by his indifference and woo women simply by existing—he is actually a pawn in everyone else's game, whether it's Machiavellian prison guard Barrows (Patrick Magee) or the slick avatar of organized crime Carter (Sam Wanamaker). For all the trappings of wealth that adorn his swinging bachelor pad, Bannion is just another working-class stiff. Like Mike, Bannion suffers an ignominious death, muttering a desperate Act of Contrition as his former accomplices search a frozen field for the loot, but Losey and Baker fail to establish Bannion as anything more than a brute, a product of a failed prison system and a slave to capitalism.

"IF YOU WANT ANYTHING IN THIS WORLD, YOU'VE JUST GOT TO GO OUT AND TAKE IT."

Baker had more success with a smaller heist movie that arrived only two years later. *A Prize of Arms* (1962) sees a trio of disgruntled former soldiers plotting to steal an army payroll before it goes overseas. Baker plays ringleader Turpin, espousing a softer take on Rave's "the good died in the war" philosophy and vaguely embittered about his dishonorable discharge following charges of black marketeering in Hamburg. *A Prize of Arms* marks a change in Baker's typecasting—Turpin is still a serious-minded criminal, but he and his crew are allowed to be likeable, not least through their struggles to complete the heist. Director Cliff Owen would make his name in comedies such as *The Wrong Arm of the Law* (1963), *A Man Could Get Killed* (1966), and two Morecambe and Wise films, and his light touch is evident here, while Paul Ryder's screenplay (based on a story by Nicolas Roeg) juggles "weak link" duties between the trio and carefully maintains tension through omission, keeping details of the heist from the audience until absolutely necessary. Were it not for the melodramatic action turn in the final act, *A Prize of Arms* could almost be considered a caper movie, with its subversive nod to the Suez Crisis and its depiction of army camp bureaucracy as both opportunity and obstacle.

"NO GUNS, NO VIOLENCE, NO ACCIDENTS..."

On August 8, 1963, a gang of criminals relieved the Glasgow-to-London mail train of over £2.3 million in used notes with minimal force. Only three of the sixteen involved managed to escape apprehension, and the others received heavy sentences for their troubles. But the men behind what was dubbed the Great Train Robbery became folk heroes at a time when Britain was beginning to kick back against the establishment. Producer Michael Deeley acquired the screen rights to Peta Fordham's

Baker's Dozen (plus one) – the "walking moustache" and the *Robbery* crew.

A concerned Joanna Pettet listens as criminal mastermind Stanley Baker contemplates a high-end heist in *Robbery*.

1965 account of the crime, *The Robbers' Tale*, hoping to set it up with director Peter Yates at Woodfall, where Deeley had been general manager. When Woodfall declined, Deeley took the project to Baker, who had enjoyed considerable success with his passion project *Zulu* three years before. Baker was extremely interested, and *Robbery* (1967) was the result.

Legal troubles had plagued earlier adaptations of the story, and so *Robbery* is a lightly fictionalized version of events, with Baker's Paul Clifton as a disguised Bruce Reynolds, the real-life ringleader. Characterization is minimal across the board, with few of the huge gang showing any particular quirks, but *Robbery* is a film about an event, not the people behind it, and its charm lies in its obsession with authentic detail. That isn't to say that *Robbery* is a dry reconstruction of events: Yates delivers some bravura set pieces, not least the opening car chase that apparently prompted Steve McQueen to hire him for *Bullitt* (1968); the location shooting by Douglas Slocombe is never less than vivid; and the script by Yates, Edward Boyd, and George Markstein is taciturn without being superficial. Baker of course is the standout performance—he is the mastermind, after all—and while some critics have called him little more than a "walking moustache," Clifton is a fine amalgamation of Baker's strengths as an actor, the quietly methodical mind working under enormous pressure. He is utterly believable as the kind of man able to put together a heist of this size, mostly because there is a part of Baker that actively admired the men who had: "I'm very proud to have been in and made *Robbery*," he said in a *Cinema* interview in 1972. "It was a good film. I think if you look at the picture closely the full message didn't get through to the audience, but there were a lot of injustices committed in my estimation with those people. I mean, they were put away for thirty years—that's just awful."

"THE MISTAKE IS TO BELIEVE THE HONESTY OF OTHERS."

Baker's decline as an actor began shortly after *Robbery*, as he was forced into unsuitable parts to mitigate the financial risk of his producing career. One of these roles is undoubtedly Mr. Graham in Peter Hall's *Perfect Friday* (1970), the deputy undermanager of the National Metropolitan Bank who decides that a life in banking is no longer for him and enlists the help of dissipated aristocrat Lord Nicholas Dorset (David Warner) and his Swiss wife, Britt (Ursula Andress), to help him swipe £300,000. On paper, *Perfect Friday* is a charming caper comedy; on film, it is anything but. Baker may relish playing against type as the stuffy bowler-hatted banker (a trope long gone by 1970), but neither he nor Andress are gifted comic actors. The arch script by Scott Forbes (based on his 1963 television play) and Anthony Greville-Bell echoes the glory days of Ealing, but requires a light touch and charisma that is sorely lacking for the most part, though intermittently glimpsed in Warner's louche Nick. Theater professional Hall doesn't help matters by using the film as an experiment in technique, insisting on oddly ostentatious zooms, flash cuts, fractured timelines, and a painfully groovy aesthetic that is as heavy-handed as Johnny Dankworth's calliope and marching band score.

"STANLEY BAKER WAS DYING, BUT HE WAS VERY MUCH ALIVE."

"I admit I'm fascinated with men who live outside the law," said Baker in 1967. "Men who rebel against the social structure; who take such terrible risks with the lives of themselves and their families." But as Anthony Storey noted in his rambling book-length profile, *Stanley Baker: Portrait of an Actor* (1977), Baker was a man who played many parts without even knowing it: actor, star, producer, husband, father. Storey's attempts to find the real Stanley Baker fail mostly because the answer is apparently so obvious: Baker was a product of his impoverished upbringing and like fellow Rhondda Valley boy Richard Burton (née Jenkins) he acted his way out of it. Burton wrote a "murderous love letter" to his old friend and rival in the *Observer* shortly after Baker's death in 1976: "He was tallish, thickish, with a face like a determined fist prepared to take the first blow, but not the second and if, for Christ's sake, you hurt certain aspects of his situation like his wife or children, or even me, you were certain to be savagely destroyed." Burton's tribute focuses on their shared background, diminishing his former understudy as a man who "read minds, not books," was "harshly unpoetic," and typecast him in death as he was in life: as a concrete-skulled tough guy who once punched a man so hard he took off an ear. ∎

J.T. WALSH
SOLID COLD

STEVE KRONENBERG

The face of the superb character actor J.T. Walsh resembled a blank canvas. But when he shifted his eyes, dropped his jaw, simulated a smirk, he could become whoever he chose to be. Like water shaped by its container, Walsh poured himself into each characterization. A quiet menace lurked behind his placid persona; he always seemed to be hiding some terrible secret. Walsh's filmography is remarkably diverse, but his talent for deception and deviance was tailor-made for the neo-noirs of the 1990s.

James Patrick Thomas Walsh was born in San Francisco on September 28, 1943. His father's military career took the youngster to Germany; by age seven, he had learned to speak that country's language fluently. As a child, Walsh toured the site of the Dachau concentration camp, an experience that would color his darkest performances. "Dad had us learning about the death camps and the atrocities," he recalled. "I believe I've used it quite a lot."

Following his father's death, Walsh returned to the United States and enrolled at the University of Rhode Island. He joined Students for a Democratic Society, organizing several anti–Vietnam War demonstrations and a sit-in at the office of the university's president. His extracurricular activities included appearances in several of the college's theatrical productions. After graduation, he worked as a VISTA volunteer, fighting to provide housing to low-income residents.

As the frustrated narc Hal Maguire, Walsh outshines a star-studded cast in *Tequila Sunrise*.

At age thirty, Walsh began to tread the boards in off-Broadway shows, using the initials "J.P." to avoid confusion with another actor. The pseudonym was misheard as "J.T." and the name stuck. Walsh balanced theater work with a variety of odd jobs before catching the eye of David Mamet, who cast him as John Williamson in the 1984 Broadway run of *Glengarry Glen Ross*. His unmannered acting style made an impression on the playwright. Walsh toiled in TV movies and daytime soaps before making his film debut as a walk-on in *Eddie Macon's Run* (1983). His versatility and malleable face were a snug fit for such comedies as *Tin Men* (1987), *Good Morning, Vietnam* (1987), and *The Big Picture* (1989). His portrayal of an arrogant congressional candidate in Sidney Lumet's *Power* (1986) was a prelude to the morally corrupt characters he'd play throughout his career.

Walsh's affinity for noir began when he reunited with Mamet for *House of Games* (1987). The writer-director tapped him for a small but pivotal role as a bystander who inadvertently stumbles onto the film's coterie of con men after they find a suitcase filled with stolen mob money. Walsh's character is the only one who votes to keep the cash: "Let's just talk about this. This money fell into our laps. Let's just face the goddamn facts." Standing amid a group of professional thieves, he does his best to keep his cool, lighting a cigarette and struggling not to break a sweat. Walsh's anonymity keeps us guessing: Is he about to get hustled—or is he part of a larger con?

With his simmering, subtle work in *House of Games*, Walsh proved he could bolster a film with the right supporting role. As a flustered and frustrated narc, he lends grit to *Tequila Sunrise* (1988), eclipsing Robert Towne's workmanlike screenplay and breezy turns from headliners Mel Gibson, Michelle Pfeiffer, and Kurt Russell. As his capital in Hollywood grew, Walsh began choosing character parts suited to his style and range. Like his idol Robert Mitchum, he'd review a script and mark the scenes in which he did *not* appear. "What I enjoy most as an actor," he once said, "is just disappearing."

In *The Grifters* (1990), Walsh does anything but disappear. He plays Cole, the king of the long con and mentor to Annette Bening's Myra Langtry. Cole is suave and satiny—until he becomes mired in paranoid delusion. "We are talking about breaking the law here," he insouciantly informs a mark, scamming his prey with an elaborate scheme that climaxes in a sham shootout with bogus FBI agents. Cole is a grandmaster of grift; Myra marvels at his smooth manner, the silken web he weaves to dupe the dopes he victimizes. But Cole's demons catch up with him. In a bravura display of unhinged madness, he ends up spreadeagled on a bed, helplessly raving and babbling before being led to a padded cell. Walsh's screen time is minimal, but his seamless shift from confident con artist to pop-eyed

King Cole: Walsh's portrayal of bipolar master con Cole is a highlight of *The Grifters*.

headbanger is a highlight of the film and an exemplar of source novelist Jim Thompson's fevered imagination. The film's director, Stephen Frears, described Walsh's style as "a plain man's hunger to get the most out of his scenes."

Walsh has a tidy role in the 1990 remake of *The Narrow Margin* (1952). He's Michael Tarlow, a crooked lawyer whose blind date with Carol Hunnicut (Anne Archer) ends in a tearful confrontation with his mob boss client (Harris Yulin). Desperation plasters Walsh's face as he begs the gangster to forgive him for absconding with a cache of cash before he's permanently silenced (Walsh would have been perfect as one of the killers hired to take out Hunnicut after she witnesses Tarlow's murder). He leaves a trail of sleaze in the noirish potboiler *Defenseless* (1991) as a seedy porn merchant whose extramarital liaisons with his attorney (Barbara Hershey) abruptly end when he's murdered and his wife (Mary Beth Hurt) is framed for the crime.

A Few Good Men (1992) is hardly a noir, but the heavy-handed military drama did give Walsh another opportunity to outshine an A-list cast while lending breadth and dimension to a key supporting role. His Lieutenant Colonel Matthew Markinson is a marine officer reluctantly conspiring to frame two young recruits for a murder ordered by Jack Nicholson's treacherous Colonel Nathan Jessup. His face furrowed by guilt and pain, Walsh imbues Markinson with conscience and contrition. His portrayal is a lesson in understatement; he deliberately paces Markinson's gradual emotional meltdown. While the picture's leads—Nicholson, Tom Cruise, and Demi Moore—play to type, Walsh digs deep to deliver an unusually poignant performance.

Hoffa (1992) reteamed Walsh with Nicholson and David Mamet. Scripted by Mamet and directed by Danny DeVito, the biopic skirts the outer edges of film noir. As glad-handing, backstabbing Teamsters Union president Frank Fitzsimmons, Walsh weaponizes his facelessness, cleverly cloaking an ambitious agenda beneath a colorless countenance. He's barely noticeable, skulking in the shadows and waiting to usurp Hoffa's hold on the union. Impassive and deceitful, Walsh's Fitzsimmons is an ideal noir antagonist.

John Dahl's *Red Rock West* (1993) offered Walsh his first substantial role in a genuine noir. He's Wayne, the big boss in small-town Red Rock, Wyoming. Mistaking an affable drifter (Nicolas Cage) for the hit man he's hired to murder his faithless wife (Lara Flynn Boyle), Walsh calmly confronts a clueless Cage with the dirty deed's details: "The best way to do this is to make it look like a simple burglary. . . well, you know what to do." When the real killer (Dennis Hopper) shows up, Dahl top-

Walsh was in his wheelhouse as sleazy porn purveyor Steven Seldes in *Defenseless*.

Phone Tag: Walsh and über femme fatale Linda Fiorentino exchange suggestive quips in *The Last Seduction*.

loads the film with a series of cyclonic twists capped by a near-perfect finale. As the film assails us with one deception after another, Wayne's slack face remains inscrutable. That evil glower he wears is a mask; we're never sure who he really is as Walsh deftly balances composure, rage, and desperation. He and Boyle share an icy chemistry, each poised to plunge a knife into the other's back. "I always thought of J.T. Walsh for the part of Wayne," Dahl recalled. "He was always prepared, always psyched, always getting to the set early." Wayne is quiet, rational, ruthless, yet Walsh infuses him with a dollop of despair, adopting the intensity and intricacy of noir's most beloved scoundrels.

Walsh has a small but notable part in *The Last Seduction* (1994), Dahl's diabolical take on the femmes fatales that haunt noir's darkest corners. As lubricious lawyer Frank Griffith, Walsh complements Linda Fiorentino's Bridget Gregory, a devious seductress who makes *Detour*'s Vera look like a Christmas angel. Frank and Bridget are two of a kind; he's her counselor (at law and at large) and her confidante. They telephonically trade jibes laced with sarcasm and spice. "Are you still an attorney?" she jabs. "Are you still a self-serving bitch?" he retorts. Screenwriter Steve Barancik has said that the film's most quoted line is uttered by Frank to Bridget: "Anyone check you for a heartbeat lately?" Some might prefer this sly exchange:

> Frank: "Are my lips moving too fast for you?"
> Bridget: "Not fast enough, as I recall."

Frank and Bridget share only phone scenes, but they've obviously shared more than phone sex. It's Frank who sets Bridget on the path to perdition, advising her to hide out in a tank town when she pilfers a wad of drug money from her abusive husband (Bill Pullman). Walsh plays Frank as a man who knows Bridget too well, a smug shyster in the tradition of Dan Duryea or Raymond Burr. Bridget knows Frank is the only man in her life whose brains are above his waist. They wink and tease long distance. If only we could see them clinch.

Black Day Blue Night (1995) is a sunbaked noir that features Walsh as Lt. John Quinn, a dogged, dog-tired detective determined to nail a transient (Gil Bellows) for robbing an armored car and killing a security guard. Walsh enriches what could have been a routine portrayal. Quinn is cynical, sick of the rote tedium of police work. We see it in his perpetual frown, his lazy stride, the way he

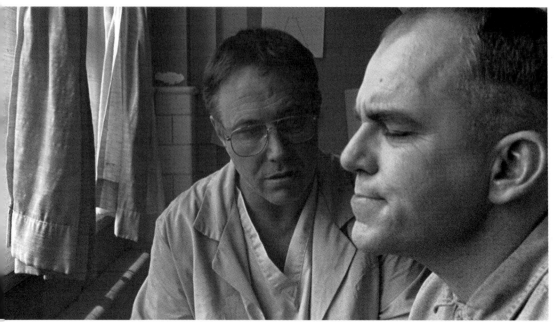

As the malignant Charles Bushman, Walsh regales Billy Bob Thornton with descriptions of depravity in *Sling Blade*.

wearily reaches for a soda in a convenience store before checking into a cheap motel. As a different kind of cop—this one crooked and crazed—Walsh single-handedly steals the convoluted noir wannabe *Persons Unknown* (1996). Some money has been snatched by a wheelchair-bound schemer (Naomi Watts) and her sister (Kelly Lynch), and the duo is soon joined by a helpful security expert (Joe Mantegna). Walsh's Cake wears his corruption on his sleeve, in the way he smokes and discards cigarettes. He purrs out a threat to Mantegna in a menacing singsong cadence: "I think your girlfriend and that pretzel in a wheelchair tried a little B&E, and if they're not dead just yet, they're gonna be real soon." The whiff of noir is unmistakable as Walsh leers at a helpless Watts in her wheelchair. "I always wanted to park in the handicapped zone," he tells her.

Walsh lobbied for the part of John Ehrlichman in Oliver Stone's *Nixon* (1995). The actor called Ehrlichman "a foil to the slavish adoration of Nixon, with the meek moral voice that would ask the questions no one else asked." Richard Nixon's rise and ruin represents both a dark chapter in history and a deep dive into real-life noir. Surrounded by a clique of coconspirators, Anthony Hopkins plays the disgraced ex-president as a crime lord reminiscent of films ranging from *Little Caesar* (1931) to *The Big Heat* (1953). As Ehrlichman, Walsh's face remains cold, almost expressionless, but he's the sole member of Nixon's cadre willing to admit that the Watergate scandal has turned his boss into a paranoid wreck. His sneer gradually becomes a scowl as he and his fellow henchmen prepare for a hard fall. In his review of *Nixon*, writer Greil Marcus labeled Walsh "the canniest and most invisible actor of the last decade."

While drafting his screenplay for *Sling Blade* (1996), Billy Bob Thornton was thinking of his friend J.T. Walsh. Thornton knew Walsh was "the only guy" for the role of Charles Bushman, a serial sexual predator confined to a psychiatric hospital along with Thornton's Karl Childers. Bushman spends his days eerily scraping a chair across a floor, parking himself beside Childers and calmly subjecting him to anecdotes about his multiple perversions. Walsh's scenes with Thornton bookend the film, but they're crucial; Thornton knew that in order to understand Childers, we must also understand Bushman. Both characters are pathologically damaged, but Bushman's dispassionate depravity is a counterpoint to Childers's vulnerability and redemption. In mere minutes, Walsh tells us all we need to know about Bushman's sadism, his casual cruelty. It's a canny performance, akin to such everyman

Breakdown breakthrough: Walsh's Red Barr captured the attention of both Kurt Russell and legions of moviegoers.

deviants as Hans Beckert in *M* (1931) and Raymond Lemorne in *The Vanishing* (1988). Thornton lauded his friend's ability to nail all his scenes in one afternoon: "The job of an actor is to portray the character that's written and portray it with all your might. J.T. did that anytime he did anything. . . . He was always perfect."

"Most bad people I've known in my life have been transparent," Walsh observed. "It's Jeffrey Dahmer arguing with the cops about a kid he's about to eat. What is the nature of evil that we get so fascinated by it? It's buried in charm, it's not buried in horror." Walsh was speaking about his signature role as toxic trucker Red Barr in *Breakdown* (1997). Jeff and Amy Taylor (Kurt Russell and Kathleen Quinlan) are traveling cross-country when their Jeep breaks down on a desert highway. Barr stops his eighteen-wheeler and offers to drive Amy to a phone. He seems amiable and trustworthy, so Amy climbs into his cab—and vanishes. Jeff gets his Jeep started and confronts Barr, who shrugs and pretends he's never seen him or his wife. Barr's lie convinces a local police officer, but he finally corners Jeff and reveals the truth: he and two cohorts (M.C. Gainey and Jack Noseworthy) have abducted Amy and are demanding a $90,000 ransom for her return. We soon learn that Amy isn't his first victim.

Russell makes a likable and resourceful hero, but *Breakdown* is Walsh's show. His portrayal of Barr is unnervingly duplicitous. He tricks us, confuses us, consistently catches us off guard. As a monster who feigns folksiness, Walsh is an actor playing an actor, a chameleonic shapeshifter with the stop-on-a-dime ability to segue from friendly to fearsome. His pliable face turns steely and sinister when he warns Jeff against retaliating. "Before you get any ideas about calling in the cavalry," he seethes, "just remember we're gonna be watching you every step of the way. And if we see anything unusual . . . well, you can just keep your fucking money, Jeff, and I'll keep your wife. And I'll mail you pieces of her from time to time." Late in the film, Barr drives his rig home and exchanges a heartfelt embrace with his adoring young son. His warmth in this scene is genuine; we nearly forget that while he's hugging his kid, he has a bound and gagged Amy inside his truck. *Breakdown* is shot in broad daylight with Walsh providing the darkness, upending our notions of villainy with a portrayal as complex as it is disturbing.

Breakdown director Jonathan Mostow was awed by Walsh's work: "He's truly the definition of

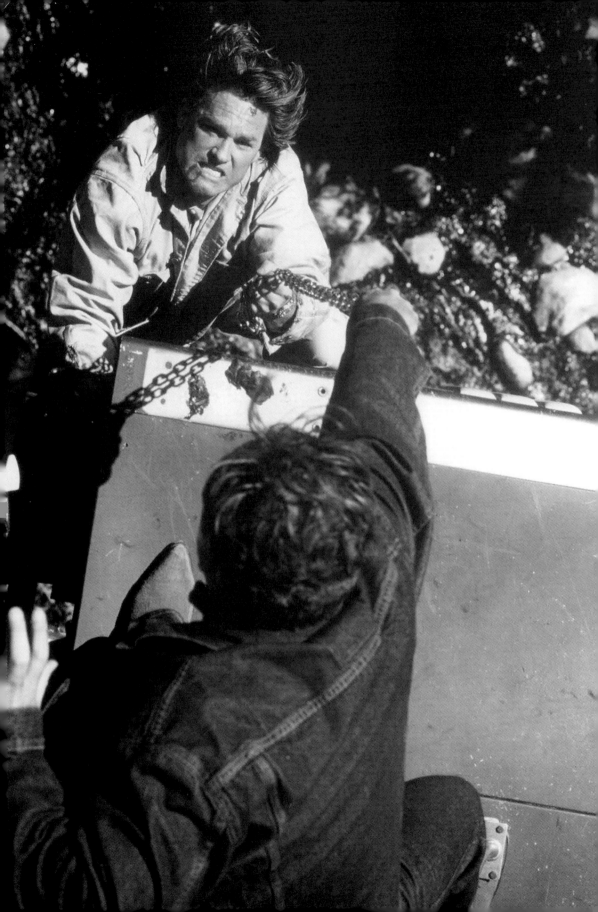

a phenomenal character actor. . . . He checks his persona at the door and disappears into his roles." Walsh had his own perspective on his penchant for playing predators. "It's fun," he declared. "I mean, what the hell, what's the choice? Or another way of putting it: Tom Cruise gets women one way. I get them another. I've just got to tie 'em up."

Breakdown was Walsh's breakthrough, affording him the widespread attention he always deserved but never received. Unfortunately, the recognition came too late. On February 27, 1998, at age fifty-four, Walsh suffered a sudden, massive, and fatal heart attack. In a lengthy article, Walsh's close friend Marc Seifer remembered him as "sincere, caring, with a great sense of humor . . . a master storyteller and also a source of wisdom." Mostow organized a memorial service for Walsh and showed the attendees a clip reel of the actor's best work. "Everyone's breath was taken away by the volume of films he'd been in," he recalled.

Walsh's versatility can be seen in such posthumously released pictures as *Pleasantville* (1998), *The Negotiator* (1998), and *Hidden Agenda* (1999). But it was the banality of evil that he honed to perfection, leaving an imprint on noir both unique and indelible. ■

(opposite) Chained for Life: Russell and Walsh are literally locked in combat during *Breakdown*'s **intense climax.**

ROLLING THE BONES FOR THE HEAVY SUGAR

By John Wranovics

It was one hell of a hat trick at the height of the noir era—*D.O.A.* (1949), *The Well* (1951), and *The Thief* (1952)—a trio of unique, high-concept thrillers borne from the brief, serendipitous collaboration of producer Harry M. Popkin, indefatigable impresario of entertainment's lower rungs, and the creative triple-threat duo of Clarence Greene and Russell Rouse.

Burlesque and boxing were where Harry M. Popkin first made bank. One guy who knew him well was Stephen "Suey" Welch, a shady East Coast prizefight manager who in 1933 had sudden reason to pursue his profession outside the United States. Headed for Australia, Welch recalled passing through California with five fighters in tow. "In Hollywood, I was grabbed as a technical director for a fight movie at Paramount. I took it, temporarily. Then a Mae West picture came up. I think I played a bit part in that. The five fighters went to work in movies, too. About that time I met Harry Popkin, the theater man."

By 1936 the *Los Angeles Times* had anointed Popkin, only thirty years old, "the Minsky of the West Coast." Born in New York, he went to high school in Toronto, where his younger brother, Leo, was born. After attending the University of California, Popkin landed a job as cashier for the Gore Brothers theater circuit in Los Angeles. He quickly built his own empire of strip joints, Burly Qs, and movie palaces, mostly in less glamorous areas of Los Angeles such as Main Street, where he operated the Burbank Burlesque Theater; South Broadway, home of his Million Dollar Theater; and Central Avenue's Lincoln Theater. By 1941, Popkin operated more than twenty-five venues.

When Suey Welch first met him, Popkin was moving into the fight game. He'd built a

gym in the basement of his Million Dollar Theater and managed Henry "King Tut" Tuttle, a veteran welterweight, in partnership with Henry Sonenshine, a fight film maker frequently in trouble with the Feds. It didn't take long, Suey recalled, for Popkin to become one of California's boxing kingpins. "We got a chance to lease the Olympic Auditorium, Dreamland in San Francisco, and the Oakland Auditorium," he said. "We promoted fights until 1937."

California's newest boxing magnate was described by one sportswriter as a "mild mannered, smart-dealing rookie in a game that has many a strange quirk." Popkin had a hard time managing those quirks, and after a couple of years of promoting fights found himself thirty thousand dollars in the hole. Welch defended Popkin, telling one reporter that he was "one of those rare sports undismayed by temporary losses—a guy who grits his teeth and shoots the works with greater vigor when the red ink flows the fastest. . . . Mr. Popkin is a gambler. To date he has been playing with 10-cent chips. So far as Dreamland is concerned, he is prepared to roll the bones for heavy sugar."

Popkin rolled too hard. In October 1938, heavyweight Alphonso "Big Boy" Bray gave the California State Athletic Commission a signed affidavit charging that Suey had offered him a thousand dollars to take a dive in his bout with Chuck Crowell at the Olympic. The CSAC pulled the team's permit and, just like that, Popkin was out of the fight game. "Harry went into producing films and I went with him, supplying talent," Suey said.

The collapse of his boxing enterprise didn't slow Popkin down one whit. Having recognized the demand for "race films" at the theaters he operated in Black neighborhoods, Popkin reinvented himself as a pioneer producer of films with all-Black casts. In May 1937, a year before the CSAC put him on ice, Harry founded the studio Million Dollar Productions. He enticed Ralph Cooper, renowned as creator and emcee of the nationally broadcast Amateur Night competition at Harlem's Apollo Theater, to sign on as the fledgling operation's marquee draw.

Harry M. Popkin built a small empire in burlesque, boxing, and B movies.

Popkin's brother, Leo, who mainly managed the Million Dollar Theater, directed the majority of the dozens of movies they produced between 1937 and 1940. Leo's willingness to shift careers was possibly spurred by the kidnapping and pistol-whipping he'd suffered a couple of months before Million Dollar Productions was launched. The papers reported three bandits had snatched him from his home, beaten him, driven him around for hours, then forced him to open the safe at the Million Dollar Theater. They got away with $1,500.

In 1994 the LA County Parks Department opened a time capsule that had been buried in the cornerstone of Castaic's Val Verde Clubhouse and Pool in 1939. Inside was a document entitled "History of Million Dollar Productions, Inc.," which declared to the people of the future that Popkin's studio "was organized May, 1937 for the purpose of producing all-colored

Popkin produced *The Duke Is Tops* (1938), the film debut of Lena Horne.

cast, modern, Class-A talking pictures with themes taken from modern Negro life." The studio's first production, *Bargain with Bullets*, a gangster picture starring Ralph Cooper, was released on September 17, 1937. According to the recovered declaration, the film "was received as the harbinger of a new era for the Negro in the portrayal of intelligent roles in Hollywood pictures."

Eventually, the Popkins and their star had a falling out, and Cooper went his own way. In 1941, with the war now underway, Million Dollar Productions closed down. In its heyday it boosted the budgets and professional quality of films made for Black audiences—as well as giving former Cotton Club chorus girl Lena Horne her first starring role in *The Duke Is Tops* (aka *Bronze Venus*) in 1938.

During the war, Harry concentrated on his theater business. The trade press noted his dedication to progressive business strategies, reporting that Popkin was "booking white acts into the Lincoln," his so-called "sepian spot," and Black acts into the Burbank (his "grind burly"). Suey Welch was identified as his booker. When the war ended in 1945, Popkin was ready to graduate to the big leagues.

RKO held the rights to Agatha Christie's 1939 novel known in the US as *And Then There Were None*. One of the great events in publishing history, with over 100 million copies sold, Christie's mystery still ranks as the fifth best-selling book of all time (right after *The Hobbit*). RKO sold the rights to famed theatrical producers the Shubert brothers, who staged Christie's play in New York with a less nihilistic finale that she had re-crafted for general audiences. In July 1944, film producer Samuel Bronston cut a deal with the Shuberts. French expat René Clair was signed to direct a film version with Dudley Nichols tapped to write its screenplay. Then Bronston got sick. And then there was no money.

The Shuberts withdrew the rights from Bronston and sold them to Popular Pictures, Inc., a company recently formed by white knights Harry M. Popkin and his new partner, Edward J. Peskay, an associate of Hal Roach and brother of an LA burlesque house operator. The press reported that six days before production was scheduled to start, "nobody had any dough," and then "a couple of

guys named Popkin and Peskay popped up and pulled the picture out of a hole." Popkin wrote the Shuberts a big check and the cameras rolled. Two years later, Bronston sued Peskay for $625,000, claiming that while incapacitated he'd hired Peskay to supervise the project's distribution and—presto chango—the venture was "secretly appropriated."

Concerned that the ending of the popular story was too well-known, the producers publicly floated the notion of filming ten different endings. Said Clair, "With just a little twist, we can pin the murders on each of the ten in ten separate endings." This gimmicky idea, though abandoned, hinted at the attention-grabbing plots Popkin would soon bring to the screen.

Now Popkin was traveling first class, with stars like Walter Huston and Barry Fitzgerald on board and a mainstream distribution deal with United Artists. When *And Then There Were None* debuted in 1945, the film was well received, winning the Golden Leopard and Best Direction Award at the 1946 Locarno International Film Festival. Popkin then rolled them bones again, forming another production company, Cardinal Pictures, and announcing that its first picture would be *Sheila*, based on a novel by Robert St. Clair.

Cardinal's first release, however, was the 1948 light comedy *My Dear Secretary*, an early Kirk Douglas effort, followed the next year by the worthy noir *Impact*, starring Brian Donlevy, Ella Raines, and Helen Walker, from a script by Jay Dratler, screenwriter of the classic *Laura* (1944). *Sheila* was once again announced as Popkin's next project, Dratler again the writer, telling a story about a woman who fights bigotry in a small California town. Hungarian cinematographer Rudolph Maté was slated to direct, with news items reporting that Maté's pact with Popkin "called for a possible second commitment, which may well be the Russell Rouse-Clarence Greene original, 'Dead on Arrival.'"

In August 1949, Popkin rolled the dice again, forming yet another production outfit, Popkin-Stiefel-Dempsey. Sam Stiefel was the manager of Mickey Rooney and Jack Dempsey, former heavyweight champion of the world. The trio announced they'd "make sports features, baseball, football, racing, boxing," and promised Dempsey would "personally supervise the production of at least one motion picture a year." But Popkin only made one film with this outfit, *The Big Wheel* (1949), an Indianapolis 500 racing story designed, like *Killer McCoy* (1947) before it, to reposition Rooney (son of Joe Yule, a veteran vaudeville performer well known in Popkin's realm) in postwar adult roles.

In 1948, 172,000 TV sets were sold in the United States. Two years later, the number rose to five million. As president of the Southern California Theater Owners Association, Popkin was acutely aware of the need for compelling stories to pull audiences into his theaters. After *The Big Wheel*, Popkin would produce only five more films before retiring from movie production. Three of those were made with the screenwriting team of Russell Rouse and Clarence Greene.

By 1949, Popkin had found his winning formula. First, attract star quality performers by offering a cut of the profits. Second, hire good writers and get out of their way. In Rouse and Greene, Harry discovered collaborators who understood the importance of ticket sales. As Popkin told a reporter, "We're trying to outguess the public. They're tired of westerns, dramas, historic epics and one world to another pictures. You gotta give them something new." Clarence Greene put it even more succinctly: "We just gotta to do something to get people out of their houses."

Russell Rouse was the third generation of his family to work in the movie business. Clarence Greene, his writing and producing partner, had practiced law in New York before giving it up to become a screenwriter. In 1951, a reporter recounted how the two had "worked for years at different studios before they met and happened to be assigned to work on the same script at one of the major studios. Their first collaboration proved a satisfactory and successful partnership and they decided to continue it." The first picture they wrote together was a now-forgotten comedy, *The Town Went Wild*

In this publicity still from *D.O.A.*, Edmond O'Brien, poked one too many times in the belly, lands one on the jaw of gun-happy Neville Brand.

In *The Well*, Henry (later, Harry) Morgan is suspect #1 in the case of a missing child that ignites a race war.

(1944), built around a young couple unwittingly headed toward an incestuous marriage.

For their first Popkin production, the duo developed the story of a man who has only forty-eight hours to live after being mysteriously dosed with "luminous poison." He races the clock against his own demise, from San Francisco to Los Angeles, in a desperate hunt for his murderer. Much of it was written while it was being filmed, often without permits on the streets of both cities.

Popkin's run-and-gun production approach enabled real-time response to actual events in the LA underworld. Rouse reported, "We've been writing the script from the day-to-day headlines," noting "when Mickey Cohen got shot at Sherry's, we worked the Sunset Strip and the outside of the nightclub into the story." Rouse told a reporter that he and Greene would "no sooner whip one development into their story than another scandal breaks." At the time of production, the LAPD was under a heavy cloud of suspicion for corruption and collaboration with gangsters. According to Rouse, "We had to convince the police department [this] was just another hunter and hunted story and didn't reflect on them." One memorable scene takes place in the landmark Bradbury Building, located just across the street from Popkin's Million Dollar Theater. Popkin cannily featured *The Big Wheel* on the marquee.

The success of *D.O.A.*, directed by Maté, inspired Popkin to create a new production unit within Cardinal Pictures, consisting of brother Leo with Rouse and Greene as writers. They announced in May 1950 that its first film would be *The Well* (referred to early on as *Deep Is the Well*). It provided Rouse his first opportunity to direct, sharing the helm with Leo, who was credited with the original story. Shot on location in Northern California, *The Well* took a neorealist approach to a story that combined a young Black girl's entrapment in a well (inspired by the 1949 Kathy Fiscus tragedy), with an *M*-like hunt for a suspected child predator, played out in a town boiling with racial tension. A frightening race riot erupts before the citizens, Black and white, come together in a desperate and suspenseful nightlong effort to save the child.

The Well was cast largely with local residents. Richard Rober, Harry Morgan, and Maidie Norman (as the missing girl's mother) were a few of the notable professional exceptions. According to Leo Popkin, "Most of the cast are housewives and ordinary businessmen. We shot *The Well* in Grass Valley in Northern California and we just went around signing up people as we needed them. We kind of told them what to do. But mostly we just turned them loose and let them do what they felt. And we got some sensational stuff." Explaining his approach, Leo claimed "I had to use people nobody'd ever seen before. . . . *The Well* is one story that would've died a quick death if I'd hired personalities you've been seeing for years and years."

The production was a turning point for Rouse and Greene, since "it gave them, in their capacity as writers, their first opportunity to see finished work appear on the screen just as they had conceived it." The Popkins were extremely supportive, and the experience, rare for screenwriters, provided Rouse and Greene "an opportunity to follow through, from the first line of the story until the film was ready for exhibition."

Released in September 1951, *The Well* received a special screening at the United Nations, after which the famed African American diplomat, Dr. Ralph Bunche, sent Harry Popkin a telegram declaring, "This is the finest motion picture ever made." Rouse and Greene were nominated for an Academy Award for Best Story and Screenplay, and Chester Schaeffer was nominated for editing. The Writers Guild of America nominated Rouse and Greene for its Robert Meltzer Award in the category "Screenplay Dealing Most Ably with Problems of the American Scene." And the Golden Globes gave Dimitri Tiomkin a nod for best original score.

Five days after *The Well* opened, a news item reported that Rouse and Greene, only two months before the film version of *A Streetcar Named Desire* was released, had traveled to Long Island—fruitlessly—to offer Marlon Brando the starring role in their next project, *The Thief*. Popkin announced that following *The Thief*, he planned to film *Serpent on the Rock*, a story inspired by the recent Iranian oil crisis. Greene and Rouse would write it, with Rouse directing. Even before *The Well* was

released, the writers "had numerous offers from major studios, but desired to operate freely under an independent setup." They stuck with the Popkins.

With *The Thief*, the Cardinal crew rolled the bones again, hard. In an effort to break through to sofa-bound TV watchers, Rouse and Greene came up with a wild idea: What if we made a ripped-from-the-headlines story about a traitorous American scientist in Washington, D.C., slipping top secret info to the Soviets? Even better, what if the movie is basically one long suspenseful chase scene, with natural sound but no dialogue? Popkin announced, "We're gonna give them a movie with no talk." To which Greene added, "Not even an 'A.'"

There was a method to their madness. Said Greene, "It's also an attempt to be progressive. We've studied many successful movies and discovered for the most part the most effective scenes . . . were without dialogue. For example, *Lost Weekend*, when Ray Milland searches for the hidden liquor. Or the finale in *Duel in the Sun*, or highly dramatic shots in *The Informer*, *The Well* and many of Hitchcock's films."

Ray Milland was tapped to star. He had his own thoughts about the advantages of going talk-free: "Dialogue is like a crutch you're used to leaning on . . . [it] can cover a multitude of sins—including bad acting." Since he also had a profit percentage of the film, the actor saw the potential financial upside, too: "Isn't it wonderful . . . we're finally making an international picture! It won't cost a dime to send out the French, Italian, Spanish or what have you version. They can even play it in Timbuktu without editing."

The press had a field day writing about how the "first talkless movie is being ground out 25 years after the industry welcomed the first 'talkie.'" They also spilled much ink on Rita Gam, in a supporting role as the sultry resident of a fleabag hotel where Milland hides out, dubbing her the "sex-without-words-girl."

The Thief opened in October 1952, but within a year the band had broken up. Rouse and Greene left the Popkins behind, ankling for a six-picture deal with Edward Small, starting with their next film, the jaw-dropping *Wicked Woman* (1953). (Rouse would marry its star, Beverly Michaels, and their son, Christopher, would sustain the Rouse legacy, going on to become an Oscar-winning film editor.)

The magical Popkin bubble had burst. Harry had some involvement in the 1954 production of *Top Banana*, basically a filmed version of the stage play. Starring Phil Silvers, *Top Banana* was shot in 3-D but released in 2-D, and it brought Popkin full circle to his burlesque roots.

Harry also tried his hand in television, backing the Dan Duryea series *The New Adventures of China Smith* (1954–56), but his feature film days were over. That didn't mean Popkin was out of angles: he rolled the bones again, this time hitting really big sugar—building an empire of drive-in theaters across the Los Angeles region. Even better, once the public's interest in drive-ins died out, the vast acreage yielded valuable and exploitable real estate.

After *The Well*, Leo C. Popkin had no further credits. He died in 2011 at the age of ninety-seven. Harry had died twenty years earlier, at eighty-five. He'd already sold the Million Dollar Theater back in 1969—for two million bucks. ■

THE NEO-NOIR WORLD OF Claude Chabrol

by Farran Smith Nehme

If you've never seen a film directed by Claude Chabrol—which is possible even for dedicated film lovers, for reasons we'll discuss—I recommend that you start as I did, with a film that came relatively late in his more-than-fifty-year career: *La Cérémonie*, from 1995.

Meet Sophie, played by Sandrine Bonnaire as a scowl given skinny life. She gets a job with the Lelièvres as a maid for their splendid mansion in Brittany. They're so gracious and cultivated, the Lelièvres, and so very, very rich. Madame Lelièvre (Jacqueline Bisset) is a dream of beauty and chic; Monsieur works at . . . well, something that has made him rich; the son is a teenage bookworm, gentle and awkward; the pretty daughter is sailing through university. Into this spotless world comes Sophie, and she is given her own room and treated with kindness. There is a dishwashing machine, but Sophie doesn't want to use it. Monsieur offers to buy eyeglasses for Sophie, who squints at anything from a grocery list to change from a cashier, but Sophie refuses. Offered driving lessons, she turns those down, too.

Alike in the darkest of ways: Sandrine Bonnaire and Isabelle Huppert in *La Cérémonie*

At first it makes no sense, this obstinate refusal to be helped, nor does the housekeeper's seething antipathy that seems to increase with each act of kindness. It isn't long before you find out what's wrong: Sophie can't read. She is not functionally illiterate, but completely so. Words on the page are so many squiggles to her. Even an eye chart is a hopeless obstacle. Concealing this fact has consumed her life. Soon Sophie meets the gum-snapping village postmistress, Jeanne (Isabelle Huppert), and Jeanne can read, all right. She does little else, and her chosen material includes the locals' personal mail. Friendly and at times pushy, Jeanne is outwardly poles apart from Sophie, but we sense they are alike in the darkest of ways. Like Sophie, Jeanne sees the Lelièvres' imperturbable happiness and comfort as a personal affront. Both women, we discover, hide violent histories behind a superficially cooperative manner.

They're all hurtling toward a brutal end; no matter how spoiler-averse you are, you know it from frame one. It's a premonition Chabrol fulfills, in spades. And more than anything, it's that sense of cruel onrushing fate that feels like film noir, or rather, the even bleaker and more violent world of neo-noir.

La Cérémonie was based—like a number of Chabrol movies—on a novel he loved, this one Ruth Rendell's *A Judgement in Stone* (1977); she in turn loved the movie. At the time the film was released, the director's lengthy and ever-gyrating career was in one of its troughs. Its smashing success announced a revival of both Chabrol and his approach to the neo-noir thriller. Throughout his life, he was most frequently compared to Alfred Hitchcock, about whom the young Chabrol cowrote a 1957 critical study with Eric Rohmer. Chabrol himself cited noir master Fritz Lang as his key influence. In truth, the Chabrol style never replicated either. Jonathan Rosenbaum, who called Chabrol "the most neglected filmmaker of the French New Wave," also wrote that "it is in the play between Hitchcock's subjectivity and Lang's objectivity that Chabrol's best work usually takes shape."

His late period, starting roughly with *La Cérémonie* and lasting up to his death, proved this. A good late Chabrol film offers all the pleasures of a crime saga but adds a frosty, decidedly left-wing view of French society and a sly, provocative wit that was all his own. The movies almost always have crime—most often a murder—but they seldom conceal a killer's identity; indeed, a Chabrol film often glories in letting you know as soon as possible who is going to cause all the trouble. The suspense lies in a clear view of the path that the characters are on, and the enforced wait to see if these people will do anything to avoid where it leads. In a Chabrol thriller, you meet characters who have no good intentions. They're on the road to hell, and in the finest tradition of any kind of noir, they're slamming the accelerator.

Claude Chabrol, born in Paris in 1930, was among the seminal group of nouvelle vague filmmakers who turned French filmmaking upside down in the late 1950s and roared through the Swingin' Sixties. Superficially his path resembles his contemporaries such as François Truffaut, Eric Rohmer, and Jean-Luc Godard, as he also began as a critic for *Cahiers du cinéma* and moved into filmmaking himself. Chabrol is credited with the inaugural film of the French New Wave: *Le Beau Serge* (1958).

But Chabrol went his own way afterward. Among his peers, he was uniquely prolific and the most commercially successful. Often called "the French Alfred Hitchcock," Chabrol was happy to swim through the cinematic mainstream. He made films in virtually every genre, but crime was Chabrol's most enduring love. Just give him a group of shifty characters, often (although not exclusively) a comfortable upper-middle-class milieu; throw in murky past deeds, some psychologically unhealthy motivations, inappropriate sexual liaisons, at least one or two good meals—and, above all, a murder, or two, or three; and Chabrol in turn would give you an irresistible watch.

With a few period-set exceptions, Chabrol did not mimic or even much reference the visual vocabulary of film noir. His style wasn't invisible, but neither was it flashy. He deployed camera movements like a resistance fighter mining a bridge—economically and with absolute precision. Critic Dave Kehr wrote, in his 2010 obituary for the man he'd considered a good friend, "He employed close-ups with discretion, as if he were declining to violate the privacy of his characters out of a concern for

Chabrol was the most prolific and commercially successful of the New Wave filmmakers.

Gérard Blain and Jean-Claude Brialy in Chabrol's *Le Beau Serge*, the inaugural film of the French New Wave. Despite starting, like Truffaut and Godard, as a critic at *Cahiers du cinéma*, Chabrol's career took a more prolific path.

bourgeois propriety." But in the movies we'll be discussing here, Chabrol can be seen using his own style to ring changes on noir themes; never merely as homage, but to push old masters' ideas in other intriguing directions.

He loved making movies, almost (some sniffed) to a fault: taking jobs for hire, using scripts that he knew were iffy, reportedly even making a movie or two because the filming would take place in a region whose cuisine he enjoyed. (Chabrol was a gourmet—the word "foodie" doesn't begin to cover it—and the pleasures and dangers of food are one of his signatures.) The result was more than fifty films over fifty years, an oeuvre with so many periods and sub-periods it's almost choose-your-own-adventure.

There is, however, a problem for an English speaker in choosing a Chabrol adventure: the availability of his films. It is, in a word, maddening. His early masterpieces *Le Beau Serge* and *Les cousins* (1959) are in the Criterion Collection; the Criterion Channel streams not only *La Cérémonie* but also the freshly relevant Vichy drama *Story of Women* (*Une affair de femmes*, 1988). But 1960's superb and controversial *Les Bonnes Femmes* is out of sight. The fantastic group of a half-dozen or so neo-noir films Chabrol made from 1968 to 1971 (often called "the Hélène cycle," after the frequent name of the female characters played by his then-wife Stéphane Audran) is not streaming, not on Blu-ray, and the few home-video versions on the market vary wildly in quality, with many sporting seasick colors and incorrect aspect ratios. *Violette Nozière* (1978)—his first collaboration with Isabelle Huppert and one of the finest films Chabrol made in any era—is in the same boat, as are other highly regarded efforts like *Les Noces rouges* (1973) and self-described "curiosities" suitable for further study, like *Les innocents aux mains sales* (1975). The reasons apparently involve tangled rights (how often must cinephiles hear that miserable refrain), and, one suspects, money, which might have amused the director—money prob-

1985's *Cop au Vin*, with Jean Poiret as Inspector Lavardin, was seen at the time as a return to form for Chabrol after a series of his periodic misfires.

lems abound in Chabrol films.

At this writing, however, the situation remains, and so, ruthlessly, like a Chabrol character, I will confine myself not only to late Chabrol, but to films that are readily available. The others I'm touching on are part of two elegant region-free boxed sets of Blu-rays from Arrow Films. "Lies and Deceit" includes *Cop au Vin* (*Poulet au vinaigre*, 1985); *Inspector Lavardin* (1986); *Madame Bovary* (an interesting 1991 adaptation with muse Huppert in the title role, but not a noir in any sense); *Betty* (1992); and *Torment* (*L'enfer*, 1994). The "Twisting the Knife" set includes *The Swindle* (*Rien ne va plus*, 1997); *The Color of Lies* (*Au cœur du mensonge*, 1999); *Nightcap* (*Merci pour le chocolat*, 2000); and *The Flower of Evil* (*La fleur du mal*, 2003, for which, full disclosure, I contributed a commentary).

The two Inspector Lavardin films from the 1980s are rather like what would happen if Lieutenant Columbo was given a savage French attitude and a far more casual set of ethics, then turned loose in the countryside to antagonize everyone in sight. In *Poulet au vinaigre* ("poulet" being slang for a cop), Lavardin (played by Jean Poiret with glinting intelligence and a decided mean streak) investigates the likely murder of a wealthy woman. He doesn't come on scene until some way into the movie, as we first meet Madame Cuno (Audran, Chabrol's wife from 1964 to 1980, and muse of the Hélène films). Madame is a shrewish, overbearing mother straight out of Hitchcock; with Freudian aplomb, she describes almost every woman who crosses her path as a "slut." Madame is pressuring her postmaster son, Louis (Lucas Belvaux), to let her steam open the village mail. The plot is tied to the desire of a trio of wealthy landowners, all of them corrupt, to buy the Cunos' dilapidated house and build some sort of ghastly development. At the time of its release, the film was regarded as a return to form for Chabrol, showing off both his macabre humor and his trademark antipathy toward the French bourgeoisie. On the surface, both *Poulet* and its somewhat less accomplished sequel are more procedural, like *Columbo*, than noir. But the rumpled TV detective never had to deal with such a loathsome array of suspects, and Lavardin's bad attitude could rival Hank Quinlan's.

The title character of *Betty*, played by the ill-fated and gifted Marie Trintignant, exemplifies another noir archetype: the hopeless drunk. Betty has, as they say in recovery parlance, hit bottom, but she's decided to set up permanent residence there. The wreckage Betty trails includes her own children, whom she's signed over to their father after years of cheating on him. Betty takes the kid-related payoff and washes up in the swank Trianon Palace hotel in Versailles. There she encounters Laure (Audran), like Betty an alcoholic, and unlike Betty, authentically rich. Laure has decided that this hotel is a fine place to spend her dwindling days and she takes Betty under her wing, not realizing that Betty's specialty is taking anything bad and making it much, much worse. Based on a novel by the reliably bleak genius Georges Simenon, this film would make my personal Chabrol top ten. It was the great Audran's last role for her former husband, and together they give Laure a final moment that is both devoid of sentimentality and crushingly sad. Chabrol, a cinephile's cinephile, called himself "a great admirer" of Billy Wilder, and Betty would play splendidly as a double feature with *The Lost Weekend* (1945), though such a bill might drive many patrons to drink.

L'Enfer (*Torment*) started its checkered life as a screenplay by Henri-Georges Clouzot, who began filming in 1964 and had to abandon the effort after a series of disasters that climaxed with Clouzot himself having a heart attack. (The whole snakebit enterprise has been memorialized in a 2009 documentary by Serge Bromberg.) The leads originally slated for Serge Reggiani (then Jean-Louis Trintignant, after Reggiani took ill) and Romy Schneider went thirty years later to François Cluzet and Emmanuelle Béart. *L'Enfer* is quite brilliant but no easy watch, forcing the viewer to spend 105 minutes with Cluzet's Paul Prieur and his inexorable descent into madness, which manifests as all-consuming sexual jealousy of his wife, Nelly (Béart).

Theoretically, audiences could have sympathy for Paul, as they do for so many unhinged characters like those played by Robert Ryan in *The Woman on the Beach* (1947) and Peter Breck in *Shock Corridor* (1963). The unusual choice for *L'Enfer* is to make Paul detestable from the moment we meet him: selfish, smug, unwilling to see anything as his own fault. Some part of Paul's unraveling

Emmanuelle Béart as *L'Enfer's* Nelly, the woman chained in marriage to Paul (François Cluzet), whose jealousy and shortcomings manifest as abuse and madness.

In *Merci pour le chocolat*, Huppert plays Mika, whose possessiveness of her husband even causes her to target stepson Guillaume (Rodolphe Pauly).

brain perceives that he doesn't merit a stone fox like Nelly, who compounds the marital imbalance by also being a decent person. But like all such people, Paul sees his inadequacy as Nelly's fault. The emotional and eventual physical abuse that he inflicts on his wife (and, because abuse always hurts the family as a whole, on his son) is the most harrowing that Chabrol had put on film since the great *La Rupture* in 1970. *L'Enfer* got some remarkably point-missing reviews on its release, notably from Roger Ebert, who wrote—infuriatingly—that Nelly must be drawn to her husband's jealousy and egging it on, because that would be more interesting than a story that had her as "a helpless bystander." The excellent commentary on the Arrow disc, by Alexandra Heller-Nicholas and Josh Nelson, neatly debunks such interpretations, discussing the techniques used by Chabrol to place events firmly in Paul's toxic head. Paul reminds me of an exchange Chabrol had with an interviewer, who remarked that Chabrol's idol Lang was fervently anti-Nazi yet fascinated by Nazis. In the same way, the journalist continued, Chabrol was fascinated by creeps. "Yes," was the director's placid reply, "because I am so strongly anti-creep." There is no creepier Chabrol character than Paul Prieur.

All four films in the second Arrow set, "Twisting the Knife," are worthwhile for a lover of noir. *The Swindle*, starring the wondrous Huppert, is a con artist comedy-thriller full of double- and triple-crosses; it forcefully suggests that criminals are capitalism's most ardent fans and able practitioners. *The Color of Lies* reunited Chabrol with Sandrine Bonnaire. Its plot focuses on an allegation of child rape and murder that leads to an atmosphere of rising hysteria in a well-to-do French village. Twenty-five years later, *The Color of Lies* prompts comparisons with our own era of so-called cancel culture.

But I'd like to focus on the last two films included, starting with *Merci pour le chocolat* (a more pleasingly appropriate and astringent title than the simple *Nightcap* used on its US release). Chabrol had an endless appetite for a good mystery novel, and this film is based on *The Chocolate Cobweb*

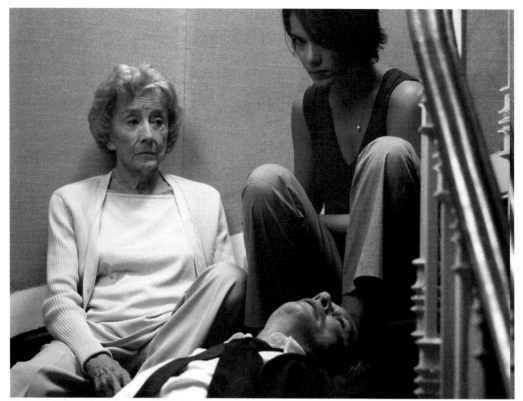

"A women's filmmaker": Suzanne Flon, left, as Tante Line and Mélanie Doutey as Michèle in *The Flower of Evil*.

(1948) by the skilled and popular Charlotte Armstrong. Unlike Armstrong, however, Chabrol is perfectly happy to leave seemingly important plot threads breezily unexplained. *Merci pour le chocolat* is set in spotless, serene, untouchably wealthy Switzerland, and concerns Mika (Huppert again), who has just remarried the concert pianist André Polonski (French singer-songwriter Jacques Dutronc) after an intervening marriage that ended in the second wife's death.

The movie shares more than a few characteristics with John Stahl's *Leave Her to Heaven* (1945), another tale of a woman consumed by the urge to destroy anything that might divide her lover's attention. Mika owns a chocolate company, but her true ownership is of André, who either doesn't perceive or can't bring himself to acknowledge her nature. Her obsession is expressed at the beginning in simple caretaking, but we figure out quite early on that Mika will crush anyone who diverts even a small portion of her husband's time and affections, and that includes his son, Guillaume (Rodolphe Pauly). It also most certainly includes interloper Jeanne (Anna Mouglalis), who discovers that due to a hospital near-switch, she might be Polonski's daughter; an intriguing idea, since Jeanne herself is a pianist of great promise. Mika is most displeased when Jeanne turns up at the family's hilltop mansion to introduce herself.

The horrifying, and at times hilarious, developments revolve around Mika's persistent and, to people either saner or less self-absorbed than Polonski and son, screamingly obvious attempts to kill anyone who gets between her and the husband, whose second wife she already bumped off. Jeanne assesses the situation pretty quickly, after witnessing a botched attempt by Mika to poison Guillaume with hot chocolate. But the boy refuses to act on Jeanne's warnings, though he obviously has some uneasiness about his stepmother. More than midway through the film, Mika surreptitiously knocks a pan of boiling water onto Guillaume's foot. Jeanne enters and Mika announces plainly, "I tipped boiling water over his foot," for all the world as if she's admitting that she dropped a fork—and this clear indication of Mika's sociopathic personality goes unremarked upon at that moment. Like the proverbial frog in a skillet, the members of Mika's household have grown accustomed to her lack of outward warmth, remorse, or indeed emotion of any kind. It's a role tailor-made for Huppert, who's often accused of being a cold actress. Chabrol understood that, on the contrary, Huppert, like Garbo, can suggest a world of roiling emotions with the merest turn of her head. Mika has her reasons, and as the movie fades and the credits roll, Chabrol and Huppert make sure we see them all.

The Flower of Evil belongs to the last decade of Chabrol's career, and some critics have described the maestro as winding down at this point; obviously, I disagree. In a 1995 interview in *Positif* around the release of *La Cérémonie*, a roundtable of journalists suggested to Chabrol that his films could be split into three eras: "The first, dominated by male protagonists, another split between Michel Bouquet and Stéphane Audran, and a third, today, when you are a women's filmmaker." Chabrol showed no displeasure at the suggestion: "A living woman, a woman who survives . . . compared to men, she is a real subject, an inexhaustible subject." *The Flower of Evil* is an especially sharp illustration of that remark.

The idea, Chabrol said, came from reading about how Lizzie Borden had lived to a ripe old age. From that he wound up spinning out a story about a wealthy family in Bordeaux who is haunted in many ways: by the deaths of two parents in an auto accident years before; by the subsequent marriage of the surviving spouses; by the affair between those spouses' children; by collaboration and murder under the Vichy regime many years before. It's a plot that in terms of mere description seems to call for a flowchart, but Chabrol focuses tightly on the human implications, and like many a tangled noir, the plot runs just fine in the background. *The Flower of Evil* gives a great final role to Suzanne Flon, who had once been the object of John Huston's passion and spent much of her career in the French theater. She plays elderly and beloved Tante Line, who years earlier had slept with her brother and murdered her collaborationist father. Yet, in typical Chabrol fashion, Tante Line is the most wholly likable person in the film; the director didn't hesitate to call her the heroine.

The Arrow sets leave off at 2002; Chabrol subsequently made four more films, all of them interesting and at least one (*The Bridesmaid*, 2004) in the front rank of his late-career output. He lived long enough to be asked about digital filmmaking (unsurprisingly, he wasn't keen). Even in the early 1980s, it was possible for a critic to describe Chabrol's career as "moving forward in a zig-zag." Chabrol, ever affable, responded, "Yes, I am an old crab. It is a way of moving that comes naturally to me." It's ironic that market forces should force us to zig-zag through a great director's filmography, but the rewards are considerable. ■

DRIVING BY NIGHT WITH PAUL ROBERTS

by Jim Thomsen

> "For every cheap hotel I've laid my head in
> For every seedy case I've tried to crack
> I'd give my weight in silver for an angel
> But when I've looked at you, you don't look back
> Trouble is my business
> Trouble is my life
> But I just don't seem to please your private eye."

—"Trouble Is My Business," Sniff 'n' the Tears, 1982

In 2011, I interviewed Paul Roberts. The British singer-songwriter had just released a new pop-rock album using the Sniff 'n' the Tears name, under which he had started his musical journey nearly four decades before. My enjoyment of those new songs sent me on a deep dive through his past music, dating back to *Fickle Heart*, the band's 1978 debut album. It's the one that spawned "Driver's Seat": one of those "oh, I love that song!" songs that has had a long second act through international TV commercials and films, most notably *Boogie Nights* (1997).

I hadn't given much thought then to Roberts as a visual artist. But in my piece, I wrote that Roberts's songs brought to mind the image of "a man of dark romantic temperament and unknowable demons, huddled in the doorway of a nightclub long after last call, hands cupped to keep his cigarette lit against a lonely wind."

Soon after, Roberts sent me an email with an image of his own: a painting of Paul Roberts, huddled in the doorway of a nightclub in the dark, hands cupped around a cigarette.

"He represented nightlife, clubs, music, glamour and the mood that I was aiming for," says Sara Rossberg, who created that oil-on-canvas image in 1983. "I do indeed see a close connection to film noir in Paul's work. There is an obvious cinematic foundation to his imagery, which often has an ominous darkness, an element of fear, unease, or the forbidden. His paintings can be suggestive of hidden events and situations, or be an actual portrayal of crime scenes. They are never ordinary."

SOMETIMES THE MUSIC came before the art, and sometimes the art came before the music. But there was no doubt that Paul Roberts was equally talented—and determined to succeed—at both.

Roberts was born in England in 1948 and raised in Wales by parents who ran a prestigious art gallery. In the early 1970s, after completing his art education, he made a splash with his photorealist, or figurative realist, paintings (labels that Roberts disdains) while writing and performing music in and around London.

He launched the first iteration of Sniff 'n' the Tears fifty years ago, having drifted in and out of a few

Paul Roberts, self-portrait, 2021

bands since his teens. After knocking around the London pub circuit for a few years with nothing to show for it but a broken heart, Roberts relocated to Paris, living in a flat too small to paint in, strumming and singing his songs in cafés and clubs along the Île Saint-Louis. A chance meeting in St. Tropez led, in a roundabout way, to the record deal that led to the recording of *Fickle Heart* in 1977 and its release in 1978 (a foreshadowing of Roberts's fickle fate in the music business).

Back in London, while waiting to see what, if anything, would come of his demo recordings, Roberts picked up his feet as a painter and attracted the patronage of prestigious London art dealer Nicholas Treadwell. His late 1970s work shows a preoccupation with Raymond Chandler and Ross Macdonald imagery: guns and cigarettes and bright lights and black shadows and dissolute dames. The painting that became *Fickle Heart*'s cover so neatly synthesizes classic elements—black cat, dead body, gun, gorgeous gams, cool metallic blues—that it's practically squeeze-tube noir concentrate.

"It was in the seventies that my love of noir developed, both in reading and in film," says Roberts, now seventy-four, from his home in Somerset, England. "I read a lot of Macdonald and I read all of Chandler. He was my gateway drug."

THE NEXT FEW YEARS for Roberts were a depressingly familiar story for any pop musician with a taste of Top 40 success. You could play Rock Star Buzzword Bingo with what happened: rushed second album, no second big single; wrong American tour strategy; wrong manager; wrong producer; constant personnel changes; et cetera, ad nauseum. All were roads leading to the dreaded "one-hit wonder" label, another that Roberts bears with bemused resignation. That term should be saved for "novelty singles," he told an interviewer. And not for careers like his, which were full of catchy, laid-back pop-rock songs that simply didn't thread the thousand jittering needles between their creation and the mass consumer consciousness the way "Driver's Seat" did.

One apparent feature that was sometimes seen as a bug: the use of Roberts's paintings on every Sniff 'n' the Tears album cover. This was particularly an issue on the band's doomed second album, when the proposed art—Roberts's 1977 painting *Hors D'oeuvre*—was deemed too prurient for the

Fickle Heart (1977), oil on canvas, by Paul Roberts

prudish American audiences craved by the band's manager, who had shepherded the band Foreigner to smash success stateside.

Said Roberts, in his online liner notes: "What had started out as an ironic pastiche of a dime-store-detective novel illustration was seen by the po-faced guardians of political correctness as a rapist's fantasy. Which I think says more about their problems than mine." (The art, ironically, was replaced by an image nearly as racy.)

The band drifted apart in 1982, and Roberts made a couple of albums under his own name that landed to little notice. By the late 1980s, Roberts—then married and the father of three girls—settled into a home-centered life balanced between art and music. He created new paintings and took the occasional commission. And he wrote new songs, releasing an album under the Sniff handle once a decade or so, and licensed his older work for commercial use.

"I FEEL LIKE I SHOULD WEAR A HAT"

A femme fatale with money by way of murder on her mind. A besotted man who wants her at any cost. A scheme developed in drowsy warmth and dappled shadows, borne out of dangerous desires and dark obsessions.

It's hard to think of a better match for the poster art of the 1981 neo-noir classic film *Body Heat* than the noir-tinged figurative realism of painter Paul Roberts.

And while Hollywood agreed, someone other than Roberts—but presuming to speak for him—did not. It's a missed brush with immortality that Roberts recalls today with more than a little body heat of his own.

"I loved the film," he says, "so yes, I was pissed off."

Roberts doesn't know all the particulars, but his recollection was that in 1979 or 1980, his sales representative at a prestigious London gallery was contacted about commissioning Roberts to produce original art for the poster of Lawrence Kasdan's film. Roberts, then busy recording and touring with Sniff 'n' the Tears, learned about the offer too late.

"He told me that there had been a request for me to do a poster for a film called *Body Heat*," Roberts says. "He said he had been to a screening and decided it wasn't for me. He didn't think, apparently, to let me be the judge of that."

Judging by his publicly displayed work up to that point, it's hard to see how *Body Heat* could *not* have been for Roberts. A look at his paintings of that era reveal a man with classic noir on his artistic mind—both in their sex-saturated subject matter and shadow-conscious style—and in a cool-metallic-blue vein consistent with the neo-noir revival of the time: Michael Mann's *Thief* (1981), the remake of *The Postman Always Rings Twice* (1981), and *Cutter's Way* (1981), among others.

(Fellow musician Kim Carnes, of "Bette Davis Eyes" fame—talk about film noir!—was so besotted with Roberts's style that she asked him to do an original cover for her 1981 album *Mistaken Identity*. When he wasn't available to do it, he says, she used one of his 1977 works in pastiche, and gave Roberts an album credit.)

The missed opportunity was, unfortunately, on a par with Roberts's bittersweet experiences in the business of music and art: "Both of my careers," he says, "have been blighted by people presuming to know what is good for me."

—*Jim Thomsen*

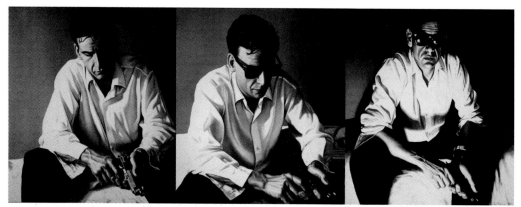

Ready, Steady, Go (1988), oil on canvas, by Paul Roberts

At about the time "Driver's Seat" was finding a lucrative second life in TV commercials, films, and CD compilations, Roberts's paintings were finding second lives on book covers. Most notably, they graced five UK reissues of George V. Higgins's crime novels, including the classics *The Friends of Eddie Coyle* (1970) and *Cogan's Trade* (1974) (the latter made into the neo-noir film *Killing Them Softly* [2012] with Brad Pitt). Other Roberts paintings have graced the covers of foreign editions of books by Alan Trustman (who wrote the screenplays for *Bullitt* [1968] and *The Thomas Crown Affair* [1968]) and Spanish author Jon Bilbao.

A commissioned work from that period shows Marilyn Monroe in night shadows and neon light, an image Roberts says was inspired by her film *Bus Stop* (1956). It's a classic example of Roberts's earliest painterly preoccupations. As he wrote in *Paul Roberts Paintings: 1977–2019*, a coffee-table book of his collected art: "My work at the time was influenced by glamour as a tool, filtered through cinema, particularly film noir, fashion photography, as well as dime-store novels and illustrations. The dream subverted."

The Bodyguard (1977), oil on canvas, Paul Roberts. The man in the background was used in pastiche for the album cover of *Mistaken Identity* (1981) by Kim Carnes.

Roberts admits to an American tilt in his tastes. It's easy to imagine them as shadowed, inversely, by his stated enjoyment of the novels of Patricia Highsmith, most of which are about lost Americans getting further lost in Europe. "I was much influenced by the panorama of the United States," he wrote in his book, "the mythology of which was central to any child growing up in Fifties or Sixties Britain."

It was a tilt reinforced by Roberts's first visit to America in 1979, when Sniff 'n' the Tears opened for Kenny Loggins and later the band Kansas on a cross-country stadium tour. With a week off at the tour's end, Roberts rented a Ford Mustang, bunked at the Sunset Marquis hotel, and took in the dissolute sights of louche, life-in-the-fast-lane LA.

"It was fascinating," Roberts says, "to me it was a mythical setting to so much that I had read or seen in the cinema." He recalls mansion parties with "large bowls of white powder for the delectation of the guests." What he calls "the aspiration in the air" inspired the lyrics to his 1980 song "Rodeo Drive": "As Donna Summer serenades the creatures of the night / Scott gets his hair just perfect and turns into the light / Then in his red Mercedes with all his moves down tight / He goes out hunting leopard in the California night."

In later years, Roberts's darkest music became more political than aesthetic. As he puts it: "As the world divides into gangster fiefdoms and the 'criminal' liberals are swept aside, reading crime fiction seems almost quaint." But echoes of his 1970s noir atmospherics still insinuated themselves into his words. That 2011 album I mentioned? Its kickoff song is "Black Money," which is, not coincidentally, the title of a Ross Macdonald novel. And its best song (in my opinion) is "Driving by Night," a thematic bookend of sorts to the fragmentary lover's despair of "Driver's Seat": "I'm threading through a highway's eye / to somewhere out of sight / Looking for adventure / in the palace of the night."

As Roberts says of the song in his online liner notes: "You may be on the A303 but you could be anywhere, driving to an assignation with a beautiful woman, or on the run from your enemies, probably the guy in the white van behind you." Sounds like someone who never lost sight of Chandler or Macdonald in the rearview mirror.

Today, Roberts remains active as a creator of new art and music, even as some of his most recent work has an air of legacy appraisal. His most recent album is an acoustic collection of songs old and new, including "Driver's Seat"; he's done a handful of two-man shows in clubs and pubs in London and the Netherlands; he passed a portion of the pandemic remixing, remastering, and rereleasing Sniff's misfired 1981 album *Love/Action* to his personal satisfaction; and he rereleased *Fickle Heart*, which was remastered for vinyl and stripped of its digital compression in accordance with its new-classic status.

And, most recently? Roberts tells me that he just completed a new "nine-minute epic" song. He adds, drily: "I have to say, it is a very noir ballad." ∎

Learn more
Paul Roberts's art: paulrobertspaintings.co.uk
Sniff 'n' the Tears: sniffnthetears.com

THE SIREN SONG OF GALE SONDERGAARD

By Steve Kronenberg

She played divas and deviants—and nearly landed the role of Hollywood's most famous wicked witch. Gale Sondergaard left an indelible imprint on every genre, from comedies to costume dramas, but her dark and diabolical demeanor was ideally suited to film noir. Her steely eyes alone could send a movie's mercury into freefall. In the 1950s her icy glare would stare down members of the House Un-American Activities Committee, daring them to imprison her for her courage and compassion.

From her birth as Edith Holm Sondergaard on February 15, 1899, in Litchfield, Minnesota, she seemed destined to conquer both the sound stage and the world stage. Her interest in acting began in high school, with a teacher who was moved to tears by Sondergaard's passionate reading of an emotional scene from *Ivanhoe*. "It's such a pity that you can't be an ordinary girl at an ordinary tea party," the woman told her. "But you can't be—you have something much more interesting to offer." Her 1917 high school yearbook presciently described her as having "the heart to conceive, the understanding to direct, and the hand to execute." She enrolled at the University of Minnesota as a drama major before securing a three-year contract with New York's renowned Theatre Guild. She bonded with her Guild colleague, actor-director Herbert Biberman, and the couple married on May 15, 1930 (they would remain wed until his death in 1971).

In addition to their passion for the arts, Sondergaard and Biberman shared a devotion to humanism and democratic ideals. Sondergaard's liberalism was forged in her formative years. "My parents were progressive people," she recalled. "My father, we thought, voted the Democratic ticket, but actually he voted the Socialist ticket. My mother was a suffragette and I marched in parades with her." Throughout her life, Sondergaard showed a strong empathy for those oppressed and exploited.

After Biberman inked a directorial deal with Columbia Pictures, the couple migrated to Hollywood, where they met and befriended director Mervyn LeRoy. Despite prodding from Biberman's agent, Sondergaard, an acclaimed Broadway performer, initially resisted the temptations of Tinseltown: "I said 'No, I don't belong in motion pictures.' I didn't think I was photogenic." Enchanted by her angular beauty and singular charm, LeRoy convinced Sondergaard to play the treacherous Faith Paleologus in the Warner Bros. costume epic *Anthony Adverse* (1936). It was an auspicious film debut; Sondergaard's Faith smiles and beguiles, her whisky-soaked whispers and sardonic smirks peppering many sluggish scenes in the film. Her performance earned her the very first Academy Award for Best Supporting Actress. "I believe Miss Sondergaard is a real find for pictures," noted producer Hal Wallis. Her versatility seemed boundless. In four comedies with Bob Hope she appeared to be in on every joke, even while playing straight to Hope's buffoonery. She fused strength with tenderness in *The Life of Emile Zola* (1937) and *Anna and the King of Siam* (1946). But she rarely strayed from cinema's dark side. Her Oscar-winning work in *Anthony Adverse* became the template for her distinctive approach to villainy in such early films as *Maid of Salem* (1937) and *Seventh Heaven* (1937).

The most famous role Sondergaard *didn't* get was offered to her in 1938 by her friend LeRoy. During preproduction for *The Wizard of Oz* (1939), LeRoy and MGM approached her to play the Wicked Witch of the West. The studio envisioned her as a beautiful but heartless sorceress, a nod both to her experience as a femme fatale and to the diabolical Wicked Queen in Disney's *Snow White and the Seven Dwarfs* (1937)—a character reportedly modeled after Sondergaard herself. Glamour shots depicted her garbed in black sequins and satin, but *Wizard of Oz* collaborator Herman J. Mankiewicz protested. "Witches should be ugly!" he declared. In an effort to conceal Sondergaard's

Sondergaard's devious Faith Paleologus sidles up to Claude Rains in this deceptively intimate scene from *Anthony Adverse*.

"Who's the Fairest of Them All?": Sondergaard rejected the role of Hollywood's wickedest witch after her proposed makeup proved too ugly for her to accept.

striking beauty, LeRoy added some disfiguring cosmetics. She balked, walked, and never looked back: "In those days I was not about to make myself ugly."

Sondergaard's snaky schemers lent brio and vivacity to all her films, but audiences were hardly prepared for her powerful work in *The Letter* (1940) as the mysterious and tormented Mrs. Hammond, whose husband is murdered by Bette Davis's Leslie Crosbie. Released shortly after *Stranger on the Third Floor* (1940), the film is both an early example of Hollywood noir and Sondergaard's first foray into the genre. Accompanied by the sound of wind chimes, she makes a grand entrance through a beaded curtain— regal, elegant, composed. Despite her enigmatic presence, her eyes and face explore a broad emotional arc: sadness, betrayal, pride, pain, rage. Her porcelain grimace briefly cracks as she tearfully gazes on the body of her murdered husband. The film's most memorable scene depicts Mrs. Hammond's confrontation with a desperate Leslie Crosbie. The scorned widow forces her captive to bow and beg for the incriminating letter she needs to preserve her alibi and escape a life in prison. Cinematographer Tony Gaudio enhances the scene's intensity, shooting Sondergaard from below as she towers over Davis's submissive form. Except for a few lines spoken in Mandarin Chinese, Sondergaard has no dialogue. She stares Davis down with an uneasy meld of contempt, fury, and heartbreak. It's a poignant and haunting performance. With only minutes of screen time, she provides the psychological and moral counterpoint to Davis's air of pretense and privilege.

Sondergaard was fully invested in Mrs. Hammond, providing invaluable insight and input into her character's dress and demeanor:

> I went to wardrobe at Warners to be fitted; before we were to begin, they brought out all these cheap, horrible things, and I said "Why would she look like that? Is it because . . . [she's] half-Chinese and not at all Caucasian?" So William Wyler, who is a marvelous director and a

marvelous man in every way said "Well, let's think about it a little." I came back the next day and he said he hadn't slept all night; he'd thought about it and he realized I was right. Why would we make her a lesser woman than the white woman? So then we began to design some gorgeous fashions which gave her dignity—which made the picture so much more interesting.

Wyler was impressed, and so was Davis. "Gale Sondergaard's performance in *The Letter* was breathtakingly sinister," Davis recalled. "I was lucky that she was cast in [the] part." Sondergaard might have disagreed with Davis's assessment. "I love that role," she said. "But I'm still shocked when people mention *The Letter* and say 'that evil role!' She was a noble woman!"

With elegance and wit, Sondergaard etched a signature portrayal in *The Spider Woman* (1944), a superior and noirish entry in Universal's Sherlock Holmes series. Drawing on the deceptively charming characters she developed in previous films, Sondergaard endows the titular and toxic Adrea Spedding with a satiny sheen and an icy heart. Her weapons are the deadly spiders she uses to dispatch wealthy suitors for their life insurance proceeds. Her allure and ingenuity are an ideal match for Basil Rathbone's Holmes. Noir fans will appreciate Spedding's visit to a seamy carnival, where she plans a fiendish demise for her persistent adversary.

Draped in black with a disarming smile, Sondergaard glides through the film, spinning her web with poise and panache, nearly seducing a smitten Holmes while both play a game of cat and mouse—or is it spider and fly? Even when apprehended, she remains cool and confident. "Elementary, my dear Holmes," she purrs. The movie is a tight sixty-three minutes, an enjoyable showcase for Sondergaard's wicked and wily style. She loved working with Rathbone and Nigel Bruce, but Adrea Sped-

Sondergaard spins an enticing web for Basil Rathbone's Sherlock Holmes in *The Spider Woman*.

ding was as much a mystery to her as she was to the master detective. "The spider woman character as scripted had no hint of background or motivations," she recollected. "And I had no concept of how to play her as a three-dimensional character. . . . Ultimately I chose to play her as Holmes' equal and allow their battle of wits to be played out much like a female Moriarty."

Christmas Holiday (1944) is an anomaly. While it begins on a yuletide weekend, it's devoid of holiday cheer. Instead, it's a disturbing exploration of maternal love gone haywire. The film boasts a malignant portrayal by Sondergaard while allowing Gene Kelly and Deanna Durbin to stretch deeply into noir. Kelly is Robert Manette, a spineless mama's boy who murders a local bookie. Durbin plays his wife, Abigail, narrating Manette's story through a series of flashbacks told to a grounded soldier (Dean Harens). Sondergaard metes out the menace as Manette's manipulative mother, willing to conceal her son's crime while denying any responsibility for his wastrel ways. The film's bleak tone is set by her subtle shifts in mood, which give the story its noir edge. Kelly plays Manette as a spoiled loser, but the film's true villain is Sondergaard's Mrs. Manette, a clinging and possessive harridan (the film hints at the pathological, semi-incestuous bond between mother and son). She sees Abigail as the mate her son needs to conquer his weakness and stand tall. "Between us, we will make him strong," she insists. Her kindly veneer soon begins to crumble. As the walls close in on Manette, his mother's smile becomes a sneer. She scapegoats Abigail in a voice laden with frost and fire: "It's I who love him because I'm willing to know all about him and keep on loving him. But *you*! I tried to make him strong myself. I couldn't alone, so I relied on you. You have failed!" Her face is cast in a quiet rage, but a closer look reveals shame and sorrow. Mother and son carry duplicity in their DNA. In the end, Manette escapes from prison, and his mother escapes culpability. When Manette is tried

Leave it to Sondergaard's malicious Mrs. Manette to ruin the yuletide for Deanna Durbin and Richard Whorf in *Christmas Holiday*.

"The Eyes Have It": Sondergaard casts a toxic spell as the title character in *The Spider Woman Strikes Back*.

and convicted for murder, Mrs. Manette's face is taut but tearless. Instead of crying, she unleashes her fury on Abigail. "*You* killed him!" she seethes, and concludes the verbal smackdown with a hard slap across Abigail's face.

The movie boasts an impressive pedigree that includes director Robert Siodmak, cinematographer Woody Bredell, and writer Herman J. Mankiewicz (adapting the 1939 novel by W. Somerset Maugham). But it's Sondergaard who steeps the picture in darkness. Even when she's not on-screen, her pernicious presence hovers over the film. *Christmas Holiday* has a few too many light moments, but Sondergaard's shadow firmly entrenches it as an essential noir.

The Spider Woman Strikes Back (1946) was intended as a follow-up for Sondergaard's Adrea Spedding, but it's a sequel in name only. Adopting only Spedding's sinister scheming, Sondergaard is renamed Zenobia Dollard, feigning blindness while plotting to steal acres of ranch land by poisoning cattle with the flowers produced by her collection of carnivorous plants. The film is a joy to watch, coupling noir-stained ambience with Sondergaard's urbane villainy. She dotes on her vampiric vegetation, plying her plants with soft, sweet whispers. *The Spider Woman Strikes Back* is a five-and-dime delight, but Sondergaard took a while to take to it. "Well, I almost had hysterics out of just hating it so," she said. "I remember it came out and people will talk about it, think it's great. . . . I've seen it and it isn't anything to be ashamed of, but I didn't like it when I did it."

In 1947, the House Un-American Activities Committee launched its Red-baiting rampage against Hollywood, demanding that actors and filmmakers "out" their liberal colleagues as communist sympathizers. Both Sondergaard and Biberman were targeted for their work with the Hollywood Anti-Nazi League and their outspoken support of the loyalists during the Spanish Civil War; HUAC pointedly ignored Sondergaard's tireless work selling war bonds during the 1940s. Refusing to cooperate with his congressional oppressors, Biberman became one of the Hollywood Ten and served a

Sondergaard's courageous testimony before the House Un-American Activities Committee consigned her to the Hollywood blacklist for twenty years.

six-month prison term for contempt of Congress. When LeRoy cast Sondergaard in *East Side, West Side* (1949), she saw it as "a test to see what the industry's reaction would be." The Hollywood establishment let out a collective hiss and blacklisted her for the next twenty years. On February 28, 1951, Sondergaard appeared before the committee and she, too, declined to be intimidated by her interrogators. Instead, she delivered a calm but impassioned speech. "I cannot but be saddened by this new offensive against the progressive conscience of Hollywood," she stated. She condemned her HUAC persecutors, called their behavior "shocking and saddening," and denounced both Hollywood and Congress for the personal affronts she suffered. "I am criticized for being a Jew-loving, Negro-loving, Red-loving, culture-loving, peace-loving, un-American woman," she declared. "It's incredible to be hated for loving so much and so many so well."

In 1969, after years of inactivity, Sondergaard triumphed in a one-woman off-Broadway show appropriately titled *Woman*. Finally released from the shackles of the blacklist, she returned to the screen in a series of low-budget features that were unworthy of her talent. During the late 1960s and early 1970s she thrived on television, appearing in everything from *It Takes a Thief* (1968–70) and *Get Smart* (1965–70) to the daytime soap *Ryan's Hope* (1975–89). In the TV movie *The Cat Creature* (1973), she reprised her sinister persona as a would-be sorceress surrounded by tarot cards and satanic symbols. When shooting wrapped, she was met by a cheering crew and Charlton Heston, who presented her with an Academy statuette to replace the plaque she won in 1937 as the first recipient of the Best Supporting Actress Oscar.

"I get great pleasure out of working, I like to create," Sondergaard said in her later years. "This is where I come alive." She bore no grudges about the blacklist and her expulsion from Hollywood.

Publishers rejected her autobiography because she wouldn't juice it up with details of those nightmare years. "I never felt bitter about what happened," she told columnist Bob Thomas. "I felt I had been a part of history, and that made me proud." The irony was bittersweet: in the 1950s she refused to betray her friends, while in the 1970s she refused to call out her enemies.

Sondergaard continued working in film and television until failing health forced her retirement and hospitalization in 1982. Following a series of strokes, she died of a cerebral hemorrhage on August 14, 1985, at the age of eighty-six. A *New York Times* obituary paid tribute to "her velvet beauty, high-arched eyebrows and broad-based smile, while managing to threaten, intimidate and terrorize the biggest stars in Hollywood." The obit didn't go far enough. On screen, Gale Sondergaard danced with the devil. Offscreen, she had the heart and soul of a saint. ■

Veronica Lake

★ CENTENARY ★

By Lynsey Ford

Veronica Lake's iconic image as the blonde bombshell with the husky purr and hourglass figure has left an indelible mark on twentieth-century popular culture. Forever known as the "Peek-A-Boo Girl" thanks to her singular hairstyle, Lake was one of the actresses who served as inspiration for the cartoon vixen Jessica Rabbit in the noir fantasia *Who Framed Roger Rabbit?* (1988). Kim Basinger delivered an Academy Award–winning performance as the high-class call girl and Lake lookalike Lynn Bracken in *L.A. Confidential* (1997). Beautiful, sultry, and unattainable, Veronica Lake had everything that a leading lady required. But Lake's private life was as tragic and convoluted as any film noir plot.

Veronica Lake was born Constance Frances Marie Ockelman in Brooklyn on November 14, 1922. She was the only child of Harry Eugene Ockelman, an employee of Sun Oil Company, and Constance Frances Charlotta (Trimble) Ockelman. Lake was nine years old when her father died in an explosion aboard an oil tanker docked in Marcus Hook, Pennsylvania. Within a year of his death, Constance married Anthony Keane, a staff artist for the *New York Herald Tribune*, and Veronica adopted her stepfather's surname. Following Keane's diagnosis of tuberculosis, the family moved to Saranac Lake in upstate New York to aid his recovery. In 1938 the Keane clan, along with Lake's cousin Helen Nelson, relocated to Beverly Hills, where Constance, an ambitious stage mother, enrolled her daughter in the Bliss-Hayden School of Acting. In Jeff Lenburg's biography *Peekaboo: The Story of Veronica Lake* (1983), Constance made the astonishing claim that acting served as a form of alternative therapy for Veronica after she was allegedly diagnosed with paranoid schizophrenia while in high school.

Lake was set to make her screen debut in RKO's *Sorority House* (1939), but her part was left on the cutting room floor. Undeterred, she appeared in a succession of frothy romantic comedies in 1939 and 1940, billed as Constance or Connie Keane when she received credit at all.

Veronica's platinum tresses and ethereal beauty caught the eye of future feature filmmaker Fred M. Wilcox (*Forbidden Planet* [1956]), then an assistant director at MGM. Citing her "natural star potential," Wilcox shot a screen test of Lake, which Lake's agent sent to producer Arthur Hornblow Jr. at Paramount. Hornblow sought an unknown to play sultry nightclub singer Sally Vaughn in his new aviation drama *I Wanted Wings* (1941). Disliking the plain "Connie Keane," Hornblow rechristened his protégé. "Veronica," according to Hornblow, reminded him of "classical features," while "Lake" complimented his discovery's navy-blue eyes, which had "the calm coolness of a lake." Veronica privately broke down at the prospect of sharing her new first name with her overbearing mother, who had been born Veronica and even listed herself as such on the 1920 census.

The Peek-A-Boo Girl

A chance moment during production of *I Wanted Wings* introduced the public to Lake's distinctive "peek-a-boo" look when her long golden locks tumbled over her right eye during a take. "I was playing a sympathetic drunk," Lake told the *New York Times* in 1969. "I had my arm on a table . . . it slipped . . . and my hair—it was always baby-fine and it had this natural break—fell over my face. It became my trademark, and purely by accident!"

Lake is sensational as Sally Vaughn, the scheming jezebel caught between best friends Jeff Young (Ray Milland), a brash, two-timing playboy, and lowly mechanic Al Ludlow (William Holden). Not only does Sally plot to ruin Jeff's career and his relationship with photographer Carolyn Bartlett (Constance Moore) with a pregnancy scare, but she also confesses to Al that she has murdered a gangster. Sally ultimately pays for her sins when she dies in a plane crash, becoming a literal "fallen woman."

Newspapers dubbed Lake "the find of 1941." *Life* magazine devoted a multipage spread to the newly minted star's mane, noting that she washed her locks in Nulava shampoo and Maro oil before rinsing them in vinegar. Millions of American women copied Lake's look, only for some to have their now-loose hair get caught in heavy machinery at their factory jobs. Lake changed her trademark coiffure at the urging of the War Manpower Commission, and encouraged working women to adopt safer hairstyles.

In 1941 Lake shot to stardom as "The Girl" in Preston Sturges's Hollywood satire *Sullivan's Travels*, opposite Joel McCrea. She followed this with five hit films in a row. *This Gun for Hire* (1942), adapted from Graham Greene's novel *A Gun for Sale* (1936), marked Lake's transition into film noir. She plays nightclub singer–magician and unlikely spy Ellen Graham, caught in the crossfire between her boss, the traitorous Willard Gates (Laird Cregar), and cold-blooded assassin Philip Raven (Alan Ladd). Irresistible in a figure-hugging evening dress, Lake makes an unforgettable entrance as Ellen, performing sleight-of-hand tricks under a luminous spotlight and Gates's intense scrutiny while singing a jazzy rendition of "Now You See It, Now You Don't." (Lake's vocals were provided by Martha Mears.) Held

Lake in *I Wanted Wings*, the film that launched her to stardom.

hostage under dark, derelict viaducts and in abandoned buildings, Ellen forges an unlikely alliance with Raven, a cat-loving psychopath damaged by childhood abuse at the hands of a sadistic aunt. Yet Ellen is also savvy enough to leave a trail of breadcrumbs for her devoted fiancé, LAPD lieutenant Michael Crane (Robert Preston), to follow, ultimately leading to Raven's grisly demise at the hands of overzealous law enforcement officers. Crane rescues Ellen, the beautiful damsel in distress punished for choosing her career over a life of domesticity, and the patriarchal order is restored.

This Gun for Hire marked the beginning of Ladd and Lake's fruitful on-screen partnership; they would costar in a quartet of films. Paramount quickly reunited the duo for *The Glass Key* (1942), the second adaptation of Dashiell Hammett's 1931 crime novel, with the studio replacing actress Patricia Morison with Lake to capitalize on her evident chemistry with Ladd. Lake's Janet Henry is the fiery daughter of gubernatorial reform candidate Ralph Henry (Moroni Olsen). She's embroiled in a tumultuous love-hate relationship with Ed Beaumont (Ladd), the right-hand man of gangster Paul Madvig (Brian Donlevy). Lake is in her element as the ruthless femme fatale who becomes Madvig's fiancée in order to secure votes for her father. It's only after the murder of her wayward brother, Taylor (Richard Denning), that the manipulative Janet reveals the darker side of her personality, recruiting Beaumont as her fellow detective while writing poison pen letters implicating Madvig in a crime he didn't commit.

Lake had become a Hollywood A-lister, receiving a weekly salary of $4,500

Lake and Alan Ladd, a potent duo for Paramount Pictures in the 1940s, first teamed in *This Gun for Hire*.

Lake's Janet Henry has political boss Paul Madvig (Brian Donlevy) wrapped around her finger in an adaptation of Dashiell Hammett's *The Glass Key*.

and four thousand fan letters a month. But as Lake's star ascended, she became susceptible to mood swings fueled by chronic alcoholism and mental illness, punctuated by hallucinations, paranoia, and dysfunctional relationships. Her tantrums and tardiness alienated her from her colleagues, and she soon earned herself a reputation for being difficult to work with. She openly feuded with Fredric March throughout the filming of *I Married a Witch* (1942). Frequent costar Eddie Bracken was unimpressed by her attitude, remarking, "She was known as 'The Bitch' and she deserved the title." Joel McCrea similarly distanced himself, allegedly commenting, "Life's too short for two films with Veronica Lake." (McCrea would make a second film with Lake, the André de Toth western *Ramrod* [1947]).

By 1943, Lake's three-year marriage to John S. Detlie was unraveling due to the pressures of fame. Detlie, a former art director at MGM, resented the role of "Mr. Veronica Lake," preferring "Ronni" to be a full-time housewife and mother to their daughter, Elaine. The couple also suffered the devastating loss of their infant son, William, who was born two months premature in 1943 after Lake tripped over a lighting cable on a film set. Lake's troubles intensified in 1944 after she publicly criticized her bosses in Boston while selling war bonds. Incensed, Paramount gave her third billing in the comedy *Out of This World* (1945). She was woefully miscast as Dora Bruckmann, a Nazi spy married to a British conscientious objector in *The Hour Before the Dawn* (1944); American audiences rejected the film, and Lake was roundly criticized for her Austrian accent. Her woes continued when she was cast in her first full-length musical *Bring on the Girls* (1945)—she didn't sing—only for the film to bomb at the box office. In 1944, Lake had also embarked on her second and longest marriage, to the self-described "Hungarian-born one-eyed cow-

Ladd and Lake reunited to great effect in *The Blue Dahlia*, which featured an original screenplay by detective-fiction writer Raymond Chandler.

boy from Texas," director André "Bandi" de Toth. She gave birth to their son, André Anthony "Michael" de Toth, in 1945, and their daughter, Diana, in 1948. But Lake eventually found herself in the thankless role of family breadwinner while de Toth pursued independent film projects.

Lake returned to Ladd's side and to form as the seductive Joyce Harwood in *The Blue Dahlia* (1946). Working from an original Raymond Chandler screenplay crackling with metaphors, wordplay, and suggestive innuendo, Lake and Ladd are mesmerizing as two drifters on the run from the law—and from marital strife with their respective spouses. Chandler detested the finished film. Cruelly referring to his leading lady as "Miss Moronica Lake," he complained about her performance, commenting that "the only times she's good is when she keeps her mouth shut and looks mysterious." Lake didn't exactly endear herself to Chandler, admitting that she didn't know who he was on set. Despite the growing froideur between the pair, *The Blue Dahlia* would earn Chandler an Oscar nomination for his script, while Lake reprised her role to acclaim opposite Ladd in a 1949 radio dramatization for the Screen Guild Theater.

Saigon (1948) marked the final Lake and Ladd pairing. In postwar China, Major Larry Briggs (Ladd), Sergeant Pete Rocco (Wally Cassell), and Captain Mike Perry (Douglas Dick) are offered $10,000 to work for shady war profiteer Alex Maris (Morris Carnovsky). When Maris is detained by police, his sexy secretary, Susan Cleaver (Lake), flies solo, carrying a suitcase containing $500,000 in cash. Following an emergency landing, the group is mistaken for smugglers while Susan is caught in a tortuous triangle between the cold, reticent Larry and Mike, the besotted, terminally ill suitor unaware that he's the odd man out. Lake and Ladd, hamstrung by a lackluster script and an implausible plot, fail to gener-

An achingly vulnerable Veronica Lake looks longingly at a duplicitous Richard Widmark in *Slattery's Hurricane*.

ate their usual chemistry as the star-crossed lovers. While critics were not kind to the film, *Saigon* fared better with audiences in the United States and abroad.

After the film's release, Paramount did not renew Lake's contract. Compounding her problems, a heavily pregnant Lake was sued by her own mother in 1948. Constance, claiming that she had spent her life savings on Lake's acting career while she herself had been reduced to relying on charity, accused Lake of failing to honor an agreement signed in 1943 stipulating that Lake would pay her $200 a week in addition to a lump sum in excess of $17,000. Lake and Constance reached a settlement in 1950, but the two women never spoke again.

Unable to secure any lucrative contracts, Lake made her final film for a major studio when she signed on with 20th Century-Fox to star in *Slattery's Hurricane* (1949). She would again be directed by her husband, with de Toth later saying that Lake's turn as a drug addict served as "shock therapy" for her. Lake is achingly vulnerable as Dolores Grieves, the brittle, neglected girlfriend of womanizing aviator Lieutenant Will Slattery (Richard Widmark). Slattery's growing obsession with his ex-girlfriend Aggie Hobson (Linda Darnell), now married to an old Navy buddy, leads Dolores to attempt suicide by overdose. Shedding her lustrous golden locks for a boyish crop, Lake delivers a beautifully understated performance as the mousy Dolores. Her heartbreak is conveyed through revealing sidelong glances as she gradually realizes the extent of Slattery's deception, and his unspoken passion for the exotic, voluptuous Aggie.

Fallen Angel

Cast adrift by Hollywood, Lake secured the lead in the independent Mexican American production *Stronghold* (1951). Lake's Maria Stevens travels to Mexico to escape the US Civil War, only to be kidnapped and caught between warring landowners Don Miguel Navarro (Zachary Scott) and Don Pedro Alvarez (Arturo de Córdova). It was, in Lake's words, "a dog," and she ended up suing Lippert Pictures to recover her salary. The creditors couldn't be kept at bay, and the IRS seized Lake's home and assets for back taxes, with the de Toths listing debts in excess of $156,500. Lake and de Toth were no longer able to sustain their lavish lifestyle, which included the services of a household staff, the use of a private plane, and the maintenance and upkeep of a twenty-three-acre ranch in Chatsworth, California.

Weary of de Toth's irresponsible spending and his jealousy, which led to accusations of infidelity while filming *Stronghold*, Lake walked out on their eight-year marriage in 1952. She relocated to New York, settling in Greenwich Village and making sporadic guest appearances on television and on the stage in the United States and the UK; in October 1955, she collapsed from exhaustion in a hotel lobby in Detroit, where she was starring in a play, and spent several weeks in the hospital. She had recently married her third husband, songwriter Joseph Allan McCarthy. Their tempestuous union was marred by domestic abuse, which culminated in a 1959 incident where McCarthy kicked Lake in the back, only for her son Michael to pull a knife on his stepfather. The couple would divorce that year.

Drifting aimlessly between a succession of cheap hotels and hostels in New York, Lake was arrested several times for being drunk and disorderly. In 1962, a *New York Post* reporter found her living in obscurity at the all-women's Martha Washington Hotel in Manhattan and working as a part-time hostess under the name Connie de Toth at the hotel's Colonnade Room cocktail bar. "I like people," she said of the job, "I like to talk to them," but the story implied that Lake was destitute. Upon its publication, fans from across the globe sent Lake letters and money, but she returned "every cent back" as "a matter of pride"—except for the thousand-dollar check from her former paramour Marlon Brando, which Lake hung on her wall instead. Often mistaken for a woman in her seventies with her sallow complexion and rotten teeth, Lake strongly denied that she was indigent, saying: "It's as though people were making me out to be down-and-out. I wasn't. I was paying $190 a month rent then, and that's a long way from being broke." The publicity surrounding her plight prompted a brief

Lake in the Canadian thriller *Footsteps in the Snow*.

career resurgence: She played the faded movie queen Gale Joy in the 1963 off-Broadway revival of the musical *Best Foot Forward*; appeared as a television hostess in Baltimore in 1966; and returned to the silver screen in a minor role in the low-budget Canadian thriller *Footsteps in the Snow* (1966). Dubbed in French, Lake plays an overprotective mother who fights to save her daughter (Meredith MacRae) from the clutches of her domineering boyfriend (Peter Kastner). *Footsteps in the Snow* wasn't released in the United States, and the film faded into obscurity.

Seeking respite, Lake traveled to Freeport in the Bahamas where she dictated her memoir to ghostwriter Donald Bain. Published in the UK in 1969 and in the United States the following year, *Veronica: The Autobiography of Veronica Lake* was universally acclaimed for its raw, unflinching honesty. In the book, reissued with a new introduction by FNF founder and president Eddie Muller in 2020, Lake candidly discussed her failed marriages, her passionate love affairs with Howard Hughes and Aristotle Onassis, the infamous "casting couch," and her fractured relationships with Constance and her estranged children. Returning to Los Angeles in 1969, she received a star on the Hollywood Walk of Fame—but was one of only three people who turned up for the ceremony. Devastated, Lake flew to the UK where she immersed herself in work, taking the lead role in the short-lived musical *Madam Chairman*, and playing Blanche DuBois in an acclaimed revival of *A Streetcar Named Desire*.

The Final Curtain

Using the proceeds from her autobiography, Lake coproduced her final film. In the abysmal *Flesh Feast* (1970), a low-budget horror movie, she plays Doctor Elaine Frederick, a mad scientist whose youth restoration formula using flesh-eating maggots is employed on an elderly patient revealed to be Adolf Hitler, still alive and residing in Miami. The film is poorly written, directed, and acted, with

Lake in 1969, one year before the release of her final film, *Flesh Feast*, which she produced herself.

Lake's stilted, wooden performance a far cry from her glory days as an alluring femme fatale.

Lake entered into her fourth and final marriage in 1972, to Robert Carleton-Munro, a captain in the British Royal Navy. The couple had filed for divorce in 1973 when Lake visited a doctor, complaining of excruciating stomach pains and nausea. She was diagnosed with cirrhosis of the liver after decades of heavy drinking; on June 26, she checked into the University of Vermont Medical Center in Burlington for further tests. Doctors initially believed that Lake would make a complete recovery. She continued to play the role of movie star from the confines of her hospital bed, signing autographs for nurses who gave her round-the-clock care.

Tragically, Lake died alone and penniless on July 7, 1973, from the effects of hepatitis and acute kidney injury. She was only fifty years old. Her son, Michael, claimed her body for cremation but had to take out a loan to pay for the cost after a bitter de Toth refused to provide any financial assistance. Veronica's old friend Donald Bain organized a modest memorial service in New York; it was sparsely attended, with none of her daughters or ex-husbands present. Her ashes remained unclaimed until March 1976 when Bain received them in the mail after he settled the funeral bill. Lake's former publicity agent William Roos scattered a portion of her ashes near the coast in Miami, where Lake had attended high school.

The formidable Constance outlived her daughter by twenty-nine years, dying at age eighty-nine in 1992. Scandal followed Lake even after death; in 2004, a teaspoon of her ashes allegedly resurfaced at an antiques store in Phoenicia, New York. It served as a sad postscript for an actress once feted as "the next Jean Harlow." Yet despite the trials and tribulations of her short, tumultuous life, Veronica Lake refused to see herself as a victim, even after she had lost everything. "There's no doubt I was a bit of a misfit in the Hollywood of the Forties," Lake admitted in her memoir. "I wanted my stardom without the usual trimmings. Because of this, I was branded a rebel at the very least. But I don't regret that for a minute. My appetite was my own and I simply wouldn't have it any other way." ■

JIM NISBET
Unleashed onto Life Itself

By Eddie Muller

One of the most unique voices in noir fiction is gone. Jim Nisbet, seventy-five, died on September 28, 2022, after a shockingly brief battle with aggressive cancer. He leaves behind fifteen novels and seven collections of poetry that earned him, at least in Europe, a reputation on par with earlier American writers such as Jim Thompson and David Goodis.

Nisbet was born in Schenectady, New York, in 1947 but relocated to North Carolina, where he studied literature at the University of North Carolina, Chapel Hill. Moving to San Francisco in the 1970s, he brought with him a distinctive drawl and hungry appreciation for the intellectual, bohemian lifestyle. While writing poetry he made his living as a carpenter, eventually becoming an in-demand creator of what he called "electronic furniture," consoles and cabinetry designed to house and enhance audio equipment.

I first encountered Jim Nisbet in 1978, when I was a student at the San Francisco Art Institute. I'd made a 16mm homage to Raymond Chandler's detective stories called Bay City Blues *and was mixing the film at Studio C, a relatively new sound house at 11th and Mission. Its co-owner, Luther Greene, loved softball even more than his thriving new enterprise, meaning clients were sought for ballplaying skill as much as filmmaking ability. One of the first teammates I'd meet was a thirty-two-year-old guy from North Carolina with thick glasses, an unruly shock of black hair, and an uproarious laugh. During postgame pizzas and beers—the first of many such seminars during my tenure as a "Mission Mugger"—I asked Jim Nisbet what he did at the studio. "I built the damn place!" he laughed.*

Nisbet was also point man for arty North Carolinians migrating to the Bay Area, back when the city was still a welcoming place for writers, artists, and musicians. I never got to know him all that well, but I can say for certain that Jim was not your average carpenter; the guy knew something about everything and even though neither of us were good ballplayers, I loved game days because, thanks to Jim, I'd always head home feeling smarter than when the day began.

Then all that ended and we went our separate ways. I didn't become the filmmaker I envisioned while hanging around Studio C. Instead, I became a writer. And twenty years passed in a flash.

I was in Larry Edmunds Bookshop in Hollywood in the spring of 2000 when a tourist from Europe overheard a conversation about film noir I was having with a couple of guys who worked there. "Are you the fellow who wrote Dark City?" *he asked. A surprise, because the book hadn't yet been published in Europe. We bantered a bit, which led to him asking, "Are you only into the films, or do you read noir fiction as well?" I assured him I did—and off to the races we went, discussing our favorites.*

Luther Greene, Richard Paige, and Jim Nisbet building Studio C

"What about Nisbet?" he asked, finally stumping me. "Do you like him?"
"Never heard of him," I said. "The only Nisbet I know is a carpenter I used to play ball with."
"I think it might be the same fellow," the guy said.

In 1984, Jim Nisbet's first novel, a wildly irreverent detective story originally entitled *The Gourmet*, was issued by fledgling publisher Black Lizard under the title *The Damned Don't Die*. The Berkeley imprint, part of Creative Arts Book Company, had been founded by author Barry Gifford principally to revive the work of forgotten writers such as Thompson, Goodis, Charles Willeford, Lionel White, Harry Whittington, and others. Gifford and Nisbet were two of the few contemporary authors Black Lizard published, and they became lifelong friends. Nisbet's subsequent Black Lizard books, *Lethal Injection* (1987) and *Death Puppet* (1989), paved the way for his future output, using the formulas of crime fiction to create story-spines on which the author brazenly grafted philosophical ruminations, keen and caustic cultural insights, and harrowing excursions into the darkest recesses of human existence.

Covers from two of Nisbet's Black Lizard novels with artwork by Jim Kirwan.

Like Gifford, Nisbet's books attracted attention from filmmakers, but unlike Gifford he never found a David Lynch (*Wild at Heart, Lost Highway*) to adapt and popularize his stories. While his first three novels were revered in Europe (Nisbet was fluent in French and translated novels and poetry), his style—unsparingly dark, unapologetically cerebral, acerbically funny, utterly unpredictable—found scant readership in America. He was, as the damned cliché goes, a "writer's writer"—provided you knew a writer who knew Jim personally and recommended his books.

A few days after I returned to the Bay Area from that trip to Hollywood in 2000, I got a call from local friend Lisa Ryan, daughter of actor Robert Ryan. We'd become pals after she'd talked to me about her dad for *Dark City*. "Have you ever heard of a writer named Jim Nisbet?" she asked. What the f&%#?

"A painter named Carol Collier wants to rent studio space from me," Lisa explained. "She's moved to San Francisco from North Carolina and is living with a local writer named Nisbet who writes crime fiction. I figured you might know him." I asked Lisa to invite Carol—and her crime-writing boyfriend—to dinner. "And invite me, too."

The shock of black hair was going gray, but the guy chugging a Tsingtao in Brandy Ho's Hunan restaurant was unmistakably my old Mission Muggers teammate.

"Hey man, I know you," we both said.
"What have you been doing the last twenty years?" we both said.
"Writing," we both said.

Amazingly, Jim Nisbet refused to let Americans' indifference to his books dampen his creativity. After a fallow period that lasted from 1989–97, his creativity reignited. Over the next ten years he fused formidable inquisitiveness with fearless imagination to create *Prelude to a Scream* (1997), *You Stiffed Me* (1998), *The Price of the Ticket* (2003), *The Syracuse Codex* (2005), *Dark Companion* (2006, nominated for the Hammett Prize by the International Association of Crime Writers), and *The Octopus on My Head* (2007), unclassifiable crime-noir-thriller-horror hybrids, mostly produced in short runs by iconoclastic publisher Dennis McMillan. Nisbet's best books maintained the dreadful momentum and mordant humor of noir while incorporating everything from metaphysics to astrophysics. Nisbet narratives routinely detoured into myriad side-subjects in which he deployed his relentless curiosity and wide-ranging intellect. He was especially adept at revealing the terror lurking within onrushing cultural trends, be it digital technology, organ transplants, homelessness, the "war on terror," or the societal chasms caused by rampant capitalism.

After the reunion at Brandy Ho's, Jim and Carol became fixtures in our lives—I'd already been married to Kathleen for fourteen years by then, and she was every bit as fond of Jim and Carol as I was. They were always the first couple on our guest list for any social engagement, whether it was a small dinner party or a backyard blowout. We regularly attended each other's public gigs, and those of our colleagues, because more than anything Jim was a loyal and fervent supporter of the arts and his friends, which were a multitude. I'd mention an artist I had recently met halfway around the world, and Jim invariably would regale me with a tale of misadventure he'd had with that person years before. Kathleen had her own memorable misadventure with Jim one night in Philadelphia, when an Asian restaurant threatened to erupt in a melee after Jim confronted a very loud Cambodian pop band booked into the same place where NoirCon was holding its annual writers' banquet. I missed the fun, sick with fever in our hotel room. But the legend lives on. You never knew what was coming next with Nisbet—on the page or in life.

Weird incidents of serendipity were part and parcel of knowing the guy. Like the time Jim came over for dinner, not long after our twenty-year reunion. I was making him a martini in the kitchen (we'd have our share over the years) and Jim started tapping a finger on a clipping stuck to the refrigerator—a page from Soap Opera Digest *that featured a photo of an old friend of mine who acted in lots of daytime TV. "Why do you have a picture of my ex-wife on your refrigerator?" Jim asked. I was incredulous. "Huh? That's my friend Dennis, who are you talking about?"*

"That may be your

Nisbet engaged in a favorite pastime — reading in the sun.

friend Dennis," Jim drawled, "but the woman in this picture with him is my ex-wife Kate." With Jim, everything was essentially two degrees of separation.

Another significant tidbit: Many years ago, I was part of a reading at M is for Mystery bookstore in San Mateo, appearing with Jim and our colleague Domenic Stansberry. The subject for the day was noir (of course), and Jim began his explanation of noir fiction with "You're fucked on page one and it's all downhill from there." I've heard that pithy description repeated endlessly since that day—never attributed to Jim Nisbet. James Ellroy, or myself, is usually credited with that line, but it was Jim.

Nisbet's outpouring of creativity continued as he entered his sixth decade, when Overlook Press republished his back catalog, as well as new work: *Windward Passage* (2010), *A Moment of Doubt* (2010), *Old and Cold* (2012), and *Ulysses's Dog* (2012, aka *The Spider's Cage*). Despite a gallant effort by publisher Peter Mayer to repackage and revitalize Nisbet's literary oeuvre, American readers remained resistant to his one-of-a-kind stories.

Snitch World (2013), published by San Francisco's Green Arcade, would end up being his final novel. It explored the dire economic and cultural changes the hi-tech gold rush wreaked on once-bohemian San Francisco, changes that would inevitably lead to the demise of Nisbet's carpentry business and spur a move from the inner city to the cramped but verdant hills of Sausalito. Jim quickly sloughed off the residual rancor, as the new digs proved to be a comfortable retreat for him, Carol, and their beloved hound, Dexter Brown Jr.

No writer was more willing to delve into the deepest, darkest parts of humanity, and himself, than Jim Nisbet. What's even more impressive is how the horror and cynicism he conjured in his writing never seeped into the enthusiasm for life that he shared with others. A ferocious amount of anger and bitterness was built into Jim's work—but like the skillful craftsman he was, he contained it on the page, exorcizing it in the words he used so dexterously and imaginatively. He absorbed all the shit and bile the world endlessly spewed out and dealt with it in his art, leaving him to live as well and as fully as anybody I've known. Jim was exactly the kind of guy an impressionable twenty-year-old wannabe artist would want as a mentor, or better yet, a lifelong friend. Man, did I luck out when he came back into my life.

Jim left a message on my phone on September 12, 2022. He did not know I was recovering from a recent medical crisis and felt too weak to talk. I didn't retrieve the voicemail for several days; he sounded robust, the only odd thing being a cryptic reference to it being "his turn." I delayed calling back because I didn't want to burden him with my woes. I'll always regret it. In my out-of-it condition, I hadn't heard the tell-tale exhaustion in his voice.

On September 28, following some final visits from friends and family, Jim succumbed to the rapidly metastasizing T-cell cancer that had caused him insufferable pain during the last weeks of his life. He died that afternoon with Carol, the love of his life, at his side.

I didn't cry when either of my parents died, but I bawled inconsolably when I learned Jim was gone. We'd never again talk and drink and share those moments of camaraderie that were so eagerly anticipated, so deeply cherished, and so terribly brief. At a loss, I spent the next day rereading his signature novel, Lethal Injection, *the tale of a burned-out doctor who assists death row executions in Texas—until he turns detective after putting down an inmate he thinks is innocent. Knowing how the doctor's quest for the truth—and Jim's—would end, I wept all the way through.*

During the pandemic quarantine Jim produced a prodigious amount of poetry,[1] much of it wry ruminations on current debacles both social and political. Jim called them "Plague Ditties," and several days after his death Carol resent to Jim's legion of friends one dated May 30, 2021, a poem timeless and profound:

No. 36

It seems to me
Said Titus Quinctius
Opening his hands to the fire

That Death releases us
Into this life
Then reclaims us

Willy-nilly, according to the rules
Of a great game
We'll never understand.

A knot popped,
Lofting a spark
Into the darkness.

A few of us, indeed,
Marcus Acilius replied,
As he drew a scrap of stone

Along the length of his blade,
Loom as if unleashed

Onto life itself,

While the majority might claim,
and not without reason,
That it's life itself

That's unleashed
On the wretched
Rest of us.

Short or tall, fat or thin
Knees unstrung by disease
Or obdurate cataclysm,

Shave your head
And get on with it —

---

1 And, I have learned from Barry Gifford, two complete novels that will, we hope, be published posthumously.

Or History will shave it for you!

Yes, muttered Quinctius,
His breath visible in the cold,
History the beancounter,

The gourmet,
The unrelenting
Custodian of death.

Selecting a length
Of bright blade at random
Acilius shaved an inch of hair

Off the back of his wrist.
Puffing the short ends
Towards the fire

With a grunt of approval,
He stood out of his cloak
And sheathed the sword,

Greaves gleaming,
Even by firelight
His scars manifest.

"Let's go."

Jim Nisbet (January 20, 1947–September 28, 2022)

INTERVIEWS
SECTION THREE

NOIR CITY
JOHN DAHL
MODERN NOIR MASTER

By Sam Moore

The 2022 recipient of the Film Noir Foundation's Modern Noir Master award, John Dahl carried the noir on his shoulders throughout the 1990s. He directed now-classics of the genre such as *Red Rock West* (1993), *The Last Seduction* (1994), and *Rounders* (1998)—an acclaimed run he credits for sustaining his career. Starting off making music videos and storyboarding for the likes of Paul Verhoeven and Jonathan Demme, Dahl was already a pro by the time of his directorial debut, *Kill Me Again* (1989). Now a director of TV shows like *Breaking Bad* (2008–13), *Justified* (2010–15), and *Dexter* (2006–13), Dahl took time out from production to talk to NOIR CITY about his life and work.

NOIR CITY: Is it true that Bill Pullman was one of your teachers at film school?
JOHN DAHL: Yes. In Bozeman, Montana, he was doing a graduate degree in theater. He came to Montana and taught. I took directing for the stage from him. He was pretty young—twenty-four, twenty-five, something like that. I got along great with him. I actually tried to get him to be in my student film, but he had the good sense to not do that. Probably the best thing that happened for Bill is that they didn't pick him up as a teacher and he moved back to New York to start acting.

NC: You started as a storyboard artist. How did you find that?
JD: I had an art background and I always liked to draw cartoons, so when I first started going to film school I thought, "Wow, I don't know anything about this, but I do know how to draw cartoons." I realized a cartoon is like a storyboard. I was trying to figure out how to make a living while I was writing scripts. I decided I would put together a résumé, and I'd sit around watching TV and drawing storyboards as quick as I could. At that time, in 1983, there was this emergence of music videos. You had all these first-time directors that had been either still photographers or graphic designers who were doing music videos. They needed storyboards, and they were willing to hire somebody who really hadn't done them before. That gave me an entry into being a storyboard artist. I was the storyboard artist on the first *RoboCop* (1987).

NC: So music videos were your way into features, similar to how directors used to get their start with Roger Corman or an exploitation movie?
JD: That's what I was hoping to do. In college, we had to write a thesis paper on a filmmaker that we admired, and everybody did the usual suspects. I did Roger Corman and my professor had no idea who he was. I assured him—this is before the Internet, so you couldn't just look people up—that he had made a lot of films. What I liked about Corman was that it was that very late '70s/early '80s do-it-yourself kind of environment. The idea of doing a Roger Corman movie appealed to me. By the time I got out of film school, it was getting pretty hard to make a Roger Corman film. But music videos came along, and nobody really knew what they were. For me, it was great. I did about three of them, and it gave me the opportunity to work with cameras, with a crew, with lighting. By the time I got on a real film set, I'd had some experience.

NC: How did you go from making those music videos to writing *Kill Me Again* and convincing the studio you could direct?
JD: When I talk to students, I always tell them the best contacts that you're ever going to have in the film business are probably sitting right next to you. That was certainly true in my case. When I was at the AFI, two guys who had been there the year before me were Steve Golin and Sigurjón Sighvatsson. They were trying to produce, doing low budget horror films. Dave Warfield and I started kind of working with them to develop scripts. We had written a horror film—I'm glad we never made this—called *Silent Night*, after the beloved Christmas carol. Then somebody actually made a movie called *Silent Night, Deadly Night* (1984), so we were trying to come up with another title for our film, throwing out ideas that involve death and killing and destruction. And we sort of stumbled on this line—kill me, kill me again. And I thought, "Oh, that's kind of hysterical, like those old pulp novels." We thought "How can we make a story out of that?" and just had to figure out a way to have somebody say "Kill me again" in the story.

NC: Was film always a big part of your life? You mentioned being a Corman fan, enjoying pulp fiction. Did you like those stories growing up?
JD: I went to the drive-in theater and *A Clockwork Orange* (1971) was playing there. I'd never seen anything like it. I took a date the first night—not a great date night movie—but I went back the next night and watched it by myself, because I'd never seen a film like that. What amazed me about that

Kilmer and Whalley were husband and wife when *Kill Me Again* was made; she was billed as Joanne Whalley-Kilmer in the film.

movie is the way they use music, the idea of putting in classical music over this violence—I'd never seen that before. Then the artwork and the wardrobe, and the design of the thing was unlike anything I'd ever seen. But I guess what excited me about that film was that somebody had to make all this artwork, somebody had to create all those things, somebody had to create this world. That stuck in the back of my head.

NC: Val Kilmer has a bit of a reputation for sometimes being difficult to work with. How did you find him, especially being a first-time director on *Kill Me Again*?
JD: That was a real education. It was interesting working with him, because he's a very talented guy. At one point he said, "You know, I'm much better when I have a character that I can kind of hide behind." If you think about the things that he did that he's best known for, it's almost like he got to play somebody else. In *Tombstone* (1993) he was fantastic and when he was Jim Morrison [*The Doors* (1991)], he's not really Val Kilmer. I was going for a naturalistic guy who's walking around a small town so I think it was a little more challenging for him, and his wife [Joanne Whalley] was also in the film. It was a complicated experience, but it was valuable. I learned a lot out of it, but it was painful. But making your first movie in Hollywood is going to be painful no matter what you do. The second movie I did, with Nicolas Cage, was a much better experience because Nic was very collaborative and interested in being there and open to what was going on. He was a guy who'd been on huge movies and *Red Rock West* is a smaller movie, but he was great.

NC: What is your general approach to actors? You've worked with such a range of them.

Double Trouble: The problems in *Red Rock West* start when amiable drifter Michael (Nicolas Cage, left) is mistaken for hit man Lyle (Dennis Hopper, right).

Friendly bar owner Wayne (J.T. Walsh) proposes to offer Michael more than a drink.

JD: My main approach is you just cast the part. I remember going up to Michael Madsen once in a scene, and I gave him a note. He said, "Okay, yeah, okay, Johnny, I got it." He did the take, and it was exactly the same as the note and it was great. Ninety percent of what an actor brings to the party is themselves anyway. You want to use their best qualities. It's like being a coach of an NBA team. You're not going to teach LeBron James how to play basketball. He already knows how to play. You just have to come up with a winning formula to make him succeed. That's really my approach to working with actors, because most of them are fantastic and they really don't need a lot of information. They just want to know if they're on the right path.

NC: *Red Rock West* has this great blend of comedy and crime. How did you balance those tones? It's a film that can be absurd but also quite nasty.

JD: I've always liked that kind of tone. It's more fun to watch a movie when it's entertaining. I watched the movie with an audience a couple of years ago and there's a whole new legion of Nicolas Cage fans, so it plays better now than it did twenty years ago. People are in on the joke with Nic. He's trying to be so focused and conscientious and get this stuff right.

NC: *Red Rock West* is about putting the most moral person in the world into the most immoral of circumstances and the dramatic absurdity of that. Are you naturally drawn to those types of Hitchcockian situations?

JD: Hitchcock was a big influence. He was so good at throwing an innocent person into a web of suspense and intrigue. That was a big influence on me as a kid. In *North by Northwest* (1959), Cary Grant is the guy in that movie and he's incredibly charming, but there's also danger and intrigue. I like movies like that. Nic is doing something similar to Cary in the movie.

NC: With *The Last Seduction*, was it true that the production company thought they were financing a softcore flick?

JD: We finished the film and they didn't really know what to do with it. I think they didn't really care. That's why it sort of fell into limbo, in terms of not getting distributed. There was one scene in a gymnasium where Bridget [Linda Fiorentino] is in a cheerleader outfit and they have sex in the gym.

I kept that to the very end of the schedule, thinking that if we went over budget I wouldn't shoot it because I didn't really think we needed to see it anyway. We filmed it on the last day and I think the people who inherited the movie thought, "Oh, we can sell this as a sexy thriller." But the sex was part of the story. They kind of left us alone. It's the film I got the least studio interference on. Pretty much everybody in Hollywood looked at that movie and decided they didn't want to release it. I'm very fortunate that audiences found (*Red Rock West* and *The Last Seduction*), as they're the reason I'm still working today as a filmmaker.

NC: Where did you find Linda Fiorentino?
JD: In our first interview, she said, "I always get these parts where I'm just the girl but what I love about this is I'm the

The Last Seduction's modern femme fatale nonpareil Bridget Gregory (Linda Fiorentino).

All in a day's work: Mike (Matt Damon) and Worm (Edward Norton) hustle the locals in Dahl's poker drama *Rounders*.

girl in the movie, but I'm actually the guy in the movie." I think it was very empowering for her to play that sort of strong female character. Linda is a very good actress. She can put on that fierce veneer, but she's also very vulnerable. You see that range nicely in the movie. She had so much fun making it; we all had fun making it. It was such a different experience, because I came onto the script with different ideas than the writer [Steve Barancik]. He thought it was more serious and I thought it was hilarious. I'd point to things in the script, like after the car wreck and she's pulling down his pants, and I'd go, "How funny and outrageous is this?" I didn't change a word of the script. I just thought it was funny.

NC: How did *Rounders* come about?
JD: I got the script, I read it, and I thought it was terrific. They also said, "We think we already have an actor for it. Matt Damon." I had never heard of him. So I went and rented some videos, and they sent me this one scene from *Good Will Hunting* (1997), and I think, "This guy's fantastic." So I met with (screenwriters Brian Koppelman and David Levien), went on a plane to New York, and three days later we started prepping. *Rounders* is now considered one of the better poker movies of all time, which is kind of exciting. Twenty years later, it is a good poker movie, because of Brian and David's approach to the script. Brian lived that story—he'd be at poker contests in Atlantic City and call Dave and say, "We gotta write a story about this." It's not a sports film, but I treated it as if it were. And I think there's a subtlety to it. Part of the charm is that it has all the slang and lingo, and the audience doesn't have to understand it to know what's happening. When I was talking to the studio, I said, "You watch a movie about a surgery and you don't know what they're talking about, but the doctors have to say all these terms if you want to make it authentic." It was the same on *Rounders*. We had to let them talk the way they talk. I think that's why it's still around. What I liked about it was the audience understood the game of poker well enough by the time you got to that last scene so that you could see what was happening. You understood that Matt had the hand and you could see him drawing out [John] Malkovich. Malkovich was great at being such a poor sport. Really fun to see him get crushed.

NC: *Joy Ride* (2001) is such a thrill, a great genre movie that really holds up. What do you think of it over twenty years later?

Dahl's father served in the Pacific during World War II, giving the director a personal reason to make *The Great Raid*.

JD: When I was casting *Rounders*, I met Steve Zahn and thought he was amazing. I liked him in the Soderbergh film he did with George Clooney, *Out of Sight* (1998). It was only a very small part, but I thought this guy's good and he's funny. He's also legitimately a great dramatic actor. One of the things that was interesting in *Rounders* is you have these two guys, and they were friends. Every guy understands what it's like to have a friend like that and to support that friend, but at some point you have to cut him loose. I think many men have male friends that they know are problematic, but we hang on to them as long as we can to try to help them. But it's a different relationship when it's your brother. I liked the fact that in *Joy Ride* they were brothers. I had heard that Steve Zahn was interested in that part, so I thought it was a great opportunity. Growing up in the West with all those big landscapes, that's a world that I know really well. I was drawn in by that, the isolation of it. You're talking about the one place in America where you can still run your car off the road and people won't ever find you if you crash in the right spot. There are no video cameras. In some places, cell phones don't work. It's still a scary, dangerous place. There are parts of the West that are so deserted there's not a person around for miles, just nothing but empty land. The Hitchcockian element of playing a practical joke and dealing with the consequences. I played a lot of practical jokes and was kind of a jerk like that as a kid. It was an interesting process because we were about to start shooting and then the studio decided they wanted to change the third act. So now we're weeks from starting shooting and we're rewriting it. Then we make the movie, they're still not happy with the ending, so we ended up shooting two or three endings. The last iteration, which is the one in the film, was the fun suspense one where we have Leelee [Sobieski] taped to a door and they're kicking the doors and if they get through that door the shotgun goes off, which I thought was a fun ride. I also liked the fact that the

Téa Leoni and Ben Kingsley in Dahl's hit-man comedy *You Kill Me*.

villain is sort of supernatural, but he wasn't. I don't really like supernatural villains because I think there's enough scary people in the world that you don't have to make them up. In the original script, Rusty Nail was disfigured somehow and that's why he was a truck driver. He didn't ever get out of this truck because he was afraid. He was this ugly guy and he thinks this woman would talk to him, but then he's completely humiliated. That eventually got left out of the story.

NC: Paul Walker is sadly no longer with us. What was he like to work with?
JD: The great thing about Paul was that a couple of days before we started, he said to me, "I'm not really an actor, I'm a surfer. I make enough money acting to keep surfing, but I think this is gonna be a fun movie to do." He was just such a charismatic, interesting guy. He was so willing to try anything, and you can't say that about every actor in Hollywood. He was one of the truly nice guys that I've ever worked with. I really enjoyed working with him. It was pretty hard to see him go. He liked doing his own stunts. He was game for all that and he was incredibly strong because he was such a great athlete. He didn't take himself very seriously, which was part of his charm as an actor and as a person.

NC: *The Great Raid* (2005) has always been interesting to me for a couple of reasons. There's that archive footage at the beginning that's quite heavy and ghastly. And it's also a depiction of the Pacific Front, which you don't see very often in film, especially compared to the Western Front. What were your motivations for making that picture?
JD: My dad is ninety-eight years old. He's a World War II veteran, and he fought in the Philippines. He's one of those quiet guys who never talks about it. When I was a kid, there was this guy who went

Dahl's lengthy TV résumé includes an early episode of *Breaking Bad* with Aaron Paul.

to our church. His name was Ben Steele. He was a survivor of the Bataan Death March. He was a kid from Roundup, Montana, and he ended up in the Philippines. When he met the medical team in the United States after spending three years in a POW camp, they said chances are you're not going to make it past the age of forty. One of the last times I saw Ben was actually on VJ Day. I happened to be in Billings and I went to the nursing home where he stayed and Ben was ninety-eight. It was a personal film.

NC: What did your dad make of the film?
JD: It was great for my dad because he came over to the Philippines and was there while we were filming. It was like an awakening for him, I think. At that time, he had loosened up on his ability to talk about World War II. It was cathartic for him in a way because he got to relive a little bit of that. At ninety-eight, he still has nightmares about being in combat. I don't think unless you've experienced that we can know what that's like. Back in the day, they didn't have post-traumatic stress disorder. You were just supposed to get on with your life and raise a family and get a job.

NC: These days you work mostly in television. Do you find it particularly different from making movies?
JD: The business has changed a lot. When I did this movie with Téa Leoni called *You Kill Me* (2007), she said, "Would you like to direct an episode of *Californication*?" which starred her then-husband David Duchovny. I thought, "Why not?" So I went and directed this episode of *Californication* (2007–14), where I didn't have to write the script. It was funny—I never get to work on comedies—and something completely different. I was done with it in two and a half weeks unlike *The Great Raid*, which took three years of my life to make. I then directed an episode of *Dexter*, then did an episode of *Battlestar Galactica* (2004–9)—so I got to go to space—and then directed an episode of *True Blood* (2008–14); it was fun to go from outer space to vampires. It reminded me of doing music videos. It was like a day job while trying to put a film together.

NC: How much creative freedom do you get on an individual episode to put your own stamp on things?

JD: You're there to help them make the best television show you can make, so the creative part is setting up shots, talking to actors, making sure that you film the story in a certain way. It's perfect for me because I'm sort of a voyeuristic filmmaker anyway, I'd rather just get the actors and photograph them as seamlessly as possible. I think my particular style works well for that world.

NC: You got to direct an episode of *Breaking Bad* before it became a huge cultural phenomenon. What was that like?

JD: I did an episode in season two and it was a fun experience. What's nice about TV directing is the problem-solving. There was a scene where [Jesse] Pinkman had his motor home taken and it was impounded in a junkyard lot. [Series creator] Vince Gilligan was there and we were scouting the location. The idea in the script was to have a junkyard dog chase Pinkman, and that was the thing stopping him from getting into his RV. But the dog was going to cost too much money, so I'm standing there and what we need is an obstacle to stop him from getting into the trailer. Right across the street was a storage yard with two hundred and fifty portable toilets. I remembered when I was in college, they would have these big festivals outside. And one time a girl was inside one of these toilets, and some asshole boys came up to it and pushed it over. This poor girl is inside with all that blue slop and all the refuse from the portable toilet is now splashed all over. So I said to Vince, "What if we put a portatoilet right next to the fence and Pinkman gets up on top, then breaks through and falls into the bottom of the toilet so he gets covered in this blue gunk?" Vince loved that idea, and that's what we ended up doing. There are so many terrific actors and writers in the business that I would rather do that than sit around and develop a screenplay for a year and a half that doesn't get made. ■

THE THIRD DEGREE
MELISSA ERRICO

Vince Keenan

NOIR CITY: Your album *Out of the Dark: The Film Noir Project* was born out of the COVID lockdown. What parallels did you see between noir and the world of the pandemic?
MELISSA ERRICO: My girls were doing remote schooling and my husband had the virus, so I locked him in the basement. That's when I fell into film noir, after midnight on YouTube. In some ways it was an escape, but in a deeper way it was a dark mirror. Estrangement, loneliness, confusion—the emotions are very similar to the ones we've all been feeling. "Ever had the feeling that the world's gone and left you behind?/Ever have the feeling that you're that close to losing your mind?" That's the way "Angel Eyes," a classic noir saloon song, begins, and I start my record with it for just that reason. It's a word-bridge between then and now.

NC: What about noir initially drew you in? What was the first movie that hooked you?
ME: In college at Yale, I took a course in film studies, where we looked at *Rififi* and I heard the title song. Of course, the professor was not drawing our attention to the music, or the cabaret aspect to it at all. The film was my first exposure to a certain kind of darkness and disturbance, so much imagery of the sordid and broken, and all entangled with the backstage world at a nightclub. A place I since know well, and have lived much of my life in—when I'm not chauffeuring children in the suburbs, that is! I fell in love with noir at that moment and swore that someday I'd sing the theme song on stage, which I got to do at the French Alliance in 2021, wearing nothing but a trench coat and broad-brimmed hat. Finding the music to that song proved very challenging, by the way. I found a sheet music copy online, in German with French subtitles.

NC: Singing "Rififi" seems like it would be difficult. But I'm not a vocalist, so what do I know?
ME: You're quite right. "Rififi" was so difficult and my first performance—oh dear, that second verse? Rapid-fire French!—was live-streamed. I had to have nerves of steel!

NC: People still argue about what makes a movie noir. What makes a song noir?
ME: One of the joys of noir is that it's a genre that was only named after it already existed. Nino Frank—see, I'm still a good little Yalie, doing my due scholarly diligence!—named it that in France, looking at three movies—*Double Indemnity*, *The Maltese Falcon*, and *Laura*—that to us don't have that much in common. Yet the current of feeling that runs through them, the sense of mystery and urban confusion, very much accented by their music, really is consistent. For me, the central symbols and themes of noir are what matter. It isn't just heartbreak, but implacable heartbreak. It isn't just being sad about love, but feeling that love was fated to never work. Those feelings—implacable fate, inevitable (and enjoyable!) oblivion, inconsolable ambivalence, the absence of obviously virtuous heroes or heroines—that's noir to me. It's why "Haunted Heart" is a noir ballad, while "Dancing in the Dark," also by Dietz and Schwartz, isn't. "Dark" is in the title, but it's essentially a happy song. "Haunted Heart" is about being haunted for life by a lover. Ravaged in the heart. So I accept and embrace neo-noir, and retro-noir, and retro-neo-noir. It's all part of one river of feeling.

NC: It's not only the songs that were chosen quite deliberately, but also the order in which they appear. What story did you want the album to tell?
ME: You're so right! There's a purposeful story arc there. It begins in a sense of fatalism and isolation—"Angel Eyes," "Written in The Stars"—then proceeds to something close to despair, as she first accepts an erotic passion ("Silent Partner"), then rejects it ("Farewell, My Lovely"), and then falls deeper into longing for the one missing man ("The Man That Got Away"). But . . . something happens. A ray of light appears. Wisdom arrives in "Shadows and Light" and hope for a getaway, a small surcease, appears in "Detour Ahead"—could there be no detour ahead? We'll drive anyway on the side of the road. And then positive affirmation at the end in "Again." It's a record of flirtation, oblivion, despair, and then final renewal. Into the dark and out of the dark.

NC: Are there preconceived notions about what noir sounds like, and if so, how do you work against them?
ME: We tried to land on songs that were familiar and make them unfamiliar. Who had heard the verse to "Angel Eyes"? Or had tried "The Man That Got Away" as an art song? We drew on the familiar sounds of noir—the poignant saxophone, the keening trumpet, the melancholy vibe—but tried to surprise even as we did.

NC: In the liner notes, you write about feeling a need "to become a femme fatale for 2021." How has that archetype evolved?
ME: My idea of the femme fatale is a little ironic—I love playing the hip-shimmying part in the special gown that the great Eric Winterling designed for me—but also more feminist than the classic kind. Of course, there was always something proto-feminist about the classic femme fatales—think of Jane Greer in *Out of the Past*, my favorite, or Rita in *Gilda*—because they had sexual autonomy. But they were a man's idea of an independent woman. Mine is more of a woman's idea. I give myself some chesty, fed-up-with-men songs to sing,

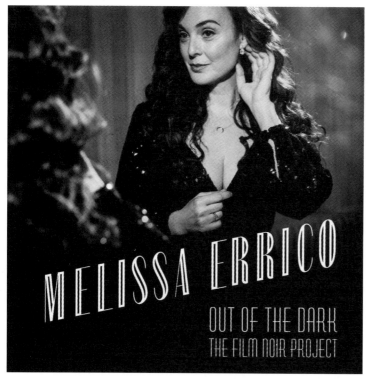

like "Checkin' My Heart," and some really crazy, active, sexual obsession songs, like Patricia Barber's "Silent Partner," which is about a woman deciding to accept an addictive erotic love, and Shire & Gopnik's "Farewell, My Lovely," which is about a woman finally saying goodbye to that same kind of erotic addiction, leaving her lover behind at dawn in a hotel room. Mine's a femme fatale who tries to control her own fate, and can laugh at her own fatality.

NC: The chanteuse has a storied history in film noir. Who are some of your favorite noir songbirds?
ME: Rita in *Gilda*, and Ida Lupino in *Road House* pro-

vided the album's finale, "Again." But I love to live in my imagination of the noir chanteuse: she's been to France, tried out in Hollywood, and is now on West 52nd Street, pouring out her broken, but not yet completely cynical, heart.

NC: The noir chanteuse does more than live in your imagination—you've created a backstory for her, which is on the album's website. Did any real-life singers inspire this character?
ME: I've always loved the sultry swing band and night club singers of that period—Julie London, Peggy Lee, June Christy, and later, Eydie Gormé. And, of course, the image of Rita Hayworth singing "Put the Blame on Mame" and Lauren Bacall not-really-singing "How Little We Know" in *To Have and Have Not* define the type. But my chanteuse is a new creation. She's a dramatic character—a little older, a little wiser, but with a perpetually surprised heart. Adam Gopnik, in the novella that accompanies the album, gave her a French background as a tribute to my love of all things French, and a Bronxville home as a wink at my actual residence. The video of "Angel Eyes" that accompanies the album is one we shot at Birdland—actual Birdland! They were kind enough to give me the club for an afternoon!—and we tried to touch on every trope of the period, from her gently loving relationship with her piano player to her weary one with the bartender, played by my friend Rufus Collins.

NC: The noir film festival you programmed emphasized French movies. Is the French version of it different?
ME: Oh, that's one of my favorite themes! If there's one thing I'm proud of in the record, it's my recording of Barbara's "Solitude." It's from much later in the period, from the 1960s, but when I suggested it the French women at FIAF nodded with exclamatory passion. She's sort of the French Joni Mitchell. Getting every syllable right in French was an ordeal, but worth it. The French sense of noir is more fatalistic than the American sense, and—can I say this?—more philosophical. American noir is about people struggling for success and never getting there; French noir is about people who know that nobody ever gets anywhere. I love the movie *Elevator to the Gallows*, where they commit the perfect murder and are betrayed by one piece of rope. Life.

NC: Talk to me about the importance of wardrobe to a femme fatale.
ME: Clothing is so important! There was no way to play a femme fatale in the wrong clothes. I could memorize Raksin songs and French noir originals until the end of time, but I could not step foot on a stage in a crappy dress. Noir is important on the inside, and crucial on the outside. I went to Eric's atelier. Blessedly, he felt the same requirement: if this is film noir, we can't mess around. After five minutes of browsing some Donna Karan loaners, Eric stopped abruptly: "I have to MAKE IT." End of story. I found the character while wearing the dress. I cannot describe it exactly, because it's a kind of ecstasy in losing myself. Full of the character's doubt and anxieties, but believing she can set others on fire. Wrapping her secrets into myself, I tie the big satin sash that holds me snug and cascades down one thigh. And I go sing my songs. You got me in the mood. Oh! When's my next concert? ∎

Out of the Dark: The Film Noir Project was released by Warner Music/Ghostlight Records in February 2022. Melissa Errico performed an encore of her noir concert at Feinstein's/54 Below in New York on May 11, 2022. This interview has been edited and condensed. —Vince Keenan

APPRECIATIONS
SECTION FOUR

PRIME CUTS: MY FAVORITE NEO-NOIR
Danilo Castro

Carlito's Way

A chronicle of a fallen criminal. A collaboration between icon Al Pacino and auteur Brian De Palma. A setting that blends American corruption with the vibrancy of Latino culture. A film that's successful in theaters but immortal on home video, where it becomes a touchstone for generations of cinephiles and sampling musicians. Not a bad formula, right? It certainly wasn't the first time, when the film was called *Scarface* and the year was 1983.

But when the same ingredients were served up as *Carlito's Way* a decade later, audiences were less impressed. Been there, done that. Who wanted a subtler take on a film that was celebrated for going so far over the top? *Carlito's Way* has a cult following today, but the perception of it as a minor rehash has mostly stayed intact. And therein lies the problem. *Carlito's Way* is *not* a lesser gangster film. It's not a gangster film at all. It bypasses the highs of *Scarface* to explore the lows of the subsequent hangover, and the result is a stealthy neo-noir classic I never tire of watching.

Al Pacino played pool in Nevada for a month to prepare for the film's tense set piece.

His friendship with Kleinfeld (Sean Penn) tests Carlito's theory about favors being deadlier than bullets.

The distinction between gangster film and noir was a crucial one for De Palma. He was reluctant to return to a milieu he'd already maximized, and only agreed to direct when he realized the source material—two novels by Edwin Torres, *Carlito's Way* (1975) and *After Hours* (1979)—was fundamentally different from *Scarface*. No longer was he dealing with a character who relished being the bad guy, but one worn down by regret and trying to make the most of a second chance. Sincerity became the operative word. The director had spent decades flirting with noir tropes through his various Hitchcock tributes, and *Carlito's Way* was a chance for him to wield his prodigious talents without relying on irony or pastiche.

David Koepp's screenplay follows suit. It rips Carlito's murder from the climax of *After Hours* and stitches it into the opening credits, emphasizing the film's debt to its 1940s predecessors. The change reframes the character's death as a foregone conclusion, and shifts focus to the humanity he managed to regain in his final months. The titular "way" becomes more pointed requiem than macho credo. From an aesthetic perspective, the opening sequence makes it doubly clear that *Carlito's Way* is the real deal. The black-and-white cinematography, floating camerawork, and bemused narration create a dreamlike experience, as though the character's transient state is dictating the form. The film establishes a groundedness (and color) once it cuts to flashback, but Carlito's narration sticks around as a reminder of impending doom.

Carlito Brigante is a big deal. Well, he used to be. He was the "J.P. Morgan of the smack business" before he was slapped with a thirty-year bid, and only the hustle of lawyer David Kleinfeld (Sean Penn) gets him out in five. Carlito's return sends waves through Spanish Harlem, but he makes it clear that his dealing days are behind him. His plan is to run a nightclub, save money, then move to the Bahamas and invest in a rental car service. "Rental car guys don't get killed that much," he reasons. Unfortunately, everybody Carlito knows is looking to either play him or pop him for his crown.

Carlito grew up idolizing Humphrey Bogart and John Garfield, even likening himself to the former in one crucial scene (following a chat with a Sydney Greenstreet counterpart, Saso, played by Jorge Porcel). The noir iconography serves a dual purpose here, highlighting not only the character's celeb-

Memory lane: Carlito returns to Spanish Harlem, weary of his reputation and the target it puts on his back.

Pacino had been attached to *Carlito's Way* since the 1980s, but the project didn't gain steam until Brian De Palma (right) was hired to direct.

rity status in the barrio, but also his dated frame of reference. He's in a time and place that no longer recognizes the merits of a personal code, and the refusal to see this simple truth puts him at a terminal disadvantage. He's an old dog bluffing his way through new tricks.

Pacino is often derided for being a caricature of his younger self, but few actors are as skilled at capturing the vitality of middle age when properly calibrated. His warm, mischievous eyes belie his weathered cheekbones. The same goes for his body language. After giving hyperverbal performances in *Scent of a Woman* (1992) and *Glengarry Glen Ross* (1992), Pacino is asked to carry long stretches of visual storytelling alone, and he does so by reaffirming his status as one of the great on-screen thinkers. Then there's the walk. Carlito might downplay his dancing, but Pacino's rhythmic stride is a thing of beauty. It bristles with angularity and purpose, mirroring the character's paranoid headspace. He can't afford to step out of line.

The film's vision of 1970s New York justifies the paranoia. The name of Carlito's nightclub, Paraiso, translates to "paradise," yet trouble is all it seems to attract. At least, under the surface. The lavish period detail, coupled with a sticky blend of disco and salsa music, makes even the most reckless behavior look mindlessly pleasurable. It's the perfect facade for a generation that crosses lines just so they can snort them. Tensions explode whenever Carlito runs afoul of this younger crowd, leading to classic De Palma set pieces like the pool hall shootout or the climactic subway chase. As Carlito weakens, however, upstarts like Benny Blanco begin to smell blood in the water.

Blanco (John Leguizamo) is the ghost of Carlito's prime. He's a pusher without a pulse, ready to do whatever it takes to get ahead. Carlito quickly pegs him as a rival, and their face-off leads to one of my favorite moments of characterization. After ordering security on a frothing Blanco, Carlito sidles up to the kid and stares him down. Blanco's face is bathed in neon red, affirming his eagerness to be the next guy up. Carlito's, meanwhile, is half white and only half red, the fury that would've led him to smite Blanco seemingly fading in real time. He lets Blanco go. Dumb move, man, dumb move. It's a wrong decision made for the right reason, the coded lighting proof that Carlito is stuck, permanently, with a foot in both worlds.

The supporting cast is similarly colorful, with actors eager to showcase their characters' compromised states. Luis Guzman instills bouncy authenticity as Carlito's bodyguard, Pachanga. He's brashly loyal, so long as there isn't a better deal around the corner. Viggo Mortensen is a model of weakness as Lalin, the wheelchair-bound con with too many questions. And then there's Penn, who commits so gleefully to the role of Kleinfeld that he nearly hijacks the film. It's a testament to his conniving performance that the lawyer winds up as the most loathsome figure in a world littered with pushers and thugs. All three betray Carlito on their way to the bottom, upending the correlation between honorless men and survival.

The only person with Carlito's best interest at heart is Gail (Penelope Ann Miller), the ballet dancer he dated before his bid. She's the "good girl" exit on his nostalgia trip, so he can't help but wince when he finds that she has fallen on hard times and resorted to stripping. This adds a neat wrinkle to an otherwise standard romance, with Carlito being forced to shed his strict outlook and embrace unpredictability. That he manages to do so for love makes his rigidity elsewhere even more tragic. Romances can often be the Achilles' heel of noir, so the fact that Gail's scenes rank as some of the film's best is a testament to their deft handling. Pacino and Miller have terrific chemistry, no doubt aided by the fact they had a real-life fling during production.

In the end, it doesn't matter who killed Carlito. A man of his stature was never going to break free. What matters is the distance he was able to put between himself and the man who created that stature. Not all the way rehabilitated, but closer than anyone thought possible. By giving Gail and their unborn son the chance to start over, the character's dream of a "new, improved Carlito Brigante" lives on. The generation gap comes back around, only here, a silver lining gleams. Maybe Charlie, Jr. will make it to *paraiso*.

Technically, Carlito's story is only a few seconds long. He recounts his entire life while waiting for his gurney to be lifted off a cracked floor, and this audacious structure illustrates why *Carlito's Way* is such a profound experience. By compressing and expanding the flow of time to match the character's perspective, the film manages to be both ephemeral and eternal. That duality keeps us noiristas entranced because it reflects our own sense of existential dread. We don't know which decision will seal our fates—or if we've already made it. We're simply passing through, hoping to make the most of our remaining cards. *Carlito's Way* may have underwhelmed back in 1993, but the film's preoccupation with (and acceptance of) impermanence is the very quality that has enabled it to stand the test of time. ■

BOOK vs. FILM
Brian Light

Moonrise, published in 1946, was already a hot property while in galley form. Everyone from Garson Kanin to John Farrow bid on the movie rights, but neophyte producer Marshall Grant ended up with them, paying fifty grand to author Theodore Strauss. Not bad for a second-time novelist whose knock-around life included an assortment of jobs: berry picker, printer's devil, road gang water boy. His first novel, *Night at Hogwallow* (1937), was a backwoods tale of a town gone wild when a white girl falsely accuses a Black man of rape.

Grant had been associate producer at Universal, breaking with the studio when it merged with International Pictures in 1946. *Moonrise* would be his first independent production, and he had landed John Garfield to star, with William Wellman directing. The project was months in development when Grant's line of credit evaporated, leaving him nearly broke. Wellman and Garfield jumped ship.

Enter Charles K. Feldman, former attorney turned agent, producer, and Hollywood enigma: "Nobody knew what he was up to," opined one obituary. Feldman brokered a deal with Republic Pictures, supplying a share of the financing in exchange for a fifty-fifty split of the profits. Grant's producing partner, Charles Haas, junked the script by Vladimir Pozner and wrote what would be the only screenplay of his career.

Feldman pitched the project to Frank Borzage. The warhorse director had recently signed a five-

Danny (Dane Clark) and Gilly (Gail Russell) framed in a dramatic, expressionistic shot.

picture deal with Republic giving him complete control of each film. Allan Dwan, Lewis Milestone, Orson Welles, Fritz Lang, and John Ford eventually made similar pacts with Republic; studio chief Herbert Yates was determined to elevate Republic's B movie reputation. Borzage's first feature for the studio, *I've Always Loved You* (1946), was the most lavish production it had ever mounted, but it ran over budget and didn't make money. Borzage, wanting out of his long-term contract, agreed to direct *Moonrise* (1948) as his final film at the studio. He and Feldman cut production costs wherever possible; despite most of the story taking place outdoors, they shot the entire film on two soundstages, as Borzage had done it in his halcyon silent days.

Many actors were considered for the lead role of Danny Hawkins including Dana Andrews, Barry Sullivan, and Fred MacMurray, but Feldman opted to borrow little-known Dane Clark from Warner Bros. A self-described "Mr. Joe Average," Clark had played bit parts at MGM under his real name, Bernard Zanville, before signing a long-term deal at Warners that included a new handle. Republic contract actress Gail Russell was cast as Gilly Johnson.

Borzage drew on the visual grammar of his silent films, driving the narrative with striking images and only selectively relying on Haas's dialogue, much of which is taken directly from Strauss's novel. The book, underpinned by themes of violence, love, and redemption, opens with this intimate tableau:

> Danny had never seen a face so speechless and yet so full of an agony to cry out. It lay back now in the tall grass at the water's edge, the neck strained as if in an effort to avoid a blow, the

mouth wide open and pulled down to one side like a man trying to scream in a nightmare, trying to scream and having no sound come out. One arm was circled above the head, the hand still squeezing a little clump of grass and root. Jerry could almost be dreaming. Only he wasn't asleep, and dead men don't have dreams.

The film's opening sequence is an expressionistic montage, set to an ominous drumbeat and shot to great effect by cinematographer John L. Russell. Stark images of a man being led to the gallows abruptly cut to a doll dangling from a noose, casting shadows over a crying infant, seamlessly linking the blood ties shared by executed father and guilt-cursed son. The dead man's walk is repeated, with the adult Danny's legs striding through the woods to a fatal confrontation with childhood nemesis Jerry Sykes (Lloyd Bridges). In the film, Danny defends himself as Jerry tries to strangle him, but in the novel, he kills in a blind rage: "A hate like lightning stabbed at Danny and at last he leaped." After delivering the deathblow Danny becomes perversely galvanized; he strides into an outdoor dance, sees Gilly being waltzed around by another man, and swoops in on her like a predator.

In both versions, Danny commandeers a car to drive Gilly home, during which flashbacks illustrate his tortured state of mind. Strauss draws the reader into Danny's fevered brain as he floors the gas pedal: "It was like running away from the world. Or maybe it was something entirely different, like running smack into it. . . . He had ninety wild horses under his foot and he was going to ride them all." When Danny climbs out of the inevitable wreck, pulling Gilly along, Borzage stages it as a figurative rebirth; Danny's initially aggressive overture toward Gilly culminates in a rain-drenched kiss—signal-

Mirror, mirror: Danny confronts his reflection as he struggles to accept his violent actions.

ing his first effort to break free of his emotional cocoon.

The novel traps the reader inside Danny's mind. The film achieves a similar effect by employing claustrophobic tight shots of his eyes, facial expressions, and physical movements. Borzage's blocking often puts Danny at odds with whomever he faces, including the town's two other "outcasts," the only people he tentatively trusts: Billy Scripture, a deaf-mute who's exiled from the townsfolk while living among them, and Mose, a Black old-timer who lives in the swamp with hunting dogs as his only company. On-screen, Danny refers to Billy (Harry Morgan) as "Dummy," but he's quick to defend Billy whenever he is teased or taunted. In Strauss's prose, Danny is even more sensitive toward Billy, referring to him by name:

> At that moment he felt a hand pull at his sleeve and turned. A blonde boy was standing there, smiling and bobbing his head with a sort of baby eagerness. But even when he smiled the boy had a sad, ageless kind of face that could have been thirteen or thirty, and the bright blue eyes had a look in them as if they were always trying to figure something out but couldn't quite make it. "Hello Billy" Danny said.

Mose (Rex Ingram, who considered this the best role ever written for a Black man), is a surrogate father to Danny, "an educated fella who's read about every book there is." Haas's script downplays the racial issues that motivated Mose to withdraw from society. Strauss had Mose say, "When I come out here, I thought I'd be out of the way and nobody would shove me around because of my color.

Danny learns that his friend and surrogate father, Mose (Rex Ingram), knows he's guilty.

Paranoia takes hold of Danny as he and Gilly ride the carnival's Ferris wheel.

What I did was resign from the human race—and I guess that's about the worst crime there is—only they don't hang you for it." The film drops the racial language; Ingram's face says it all.

The movie's narrative hews closely to the book. When hounds find Jerry's body, Danny angrily kicks Mose's dog to distract the hunters. The perceptive Mose sees through this misplaced aggression. "Ain't no reason to kick the dog," he prods Danny. "She didn't kill Jerry Sykes." The town's sheriff, Clem Otis (Allyn Joslyn, in a role initially slated for Art Smith), steps right out of the novel. He conducts his investigation using keen observations and homespun reflections: "Shucks, I can catch me a criminal quicker just going along Main Street and listening than I can with a pack of bloodhounds." When Otis pegs a gambler who held a voucher on Sykes as the prime suspect in the killing, Danny feels safe enough to abandon clandestine meetings with Gilly—once Jerry's girl—and squire her to the town fair.

> So far no one had recognized them, nobody even said hello. It was as if being part of the crowd had given him a disguise, and Danny had a sudden, wonderful feeling that this was what the world was like, a world where everybody wore a disguise. Everybody, it seemed like, was something else than what they looked like—liars, beggars, clowns, thieves, murderers, freaks. Everybody was guilty of something, and because of that nobody was more guilty than anyone else.

In both versions, this cynicism gnaws at Danny. The sequence on the Ferris wheel, full of jagged editing and vertiginous camera angles, is a bravura visual display of paranoia. The optical effects for this (and the film's opening sequence) were supplied by brothers Howard and Theodore Lydecker, who brought their special effects wizardry to more than three hundred pictures.

Strauss only deviates from Danny's POV twice—as does the film—first to take the reader through "a day in the life" of Billy Scripture, which is *every day* of Billy's isolated life. After being gently ushered out of the hardware store at closing time, Billy limps through town mourning the passing of another day: "Night was a defeat he could not understand. It came down like the sudden and vexatious lowering of a curtain." Heading home, Billy stops, as he does every night, to stand on a pair of shoe prints in the concrete sidewalk:

> It was a long time now since his own foot had fitted the impression, and all he could do now was stand on it. But even just standing there he was filled with a curious assurance and pride, something private, a secret that was always there. But it was a secret whose meaning he had forgotten just as he had forgotten the print was the print of his own foot. . . . Billy's mind was full of secrets like that, secrets without meaning.

The film distills Billy's "long day's journey into night" down to just the footprint, and Morgan imbues the scene and the ensuing altercation with Danny (taken directly from the novel) with aching sadness.

Strauss then shifts to Sheriff Otis's POV as he muses on murder and other topics with the jaundiced town coroner. "It takes two to commit it—the killer and the killed, the man who hates and the man who's hated. Sometimes I think that if you were to go into all the reasons why that rock struck Jerry Sykes's head you might wind up writing the history of the world."

In the novel, Otis tumbles to Danny's guilt and tries to force his hand by bringing Billy in for questioning. But Danny's already in the wind. The film's climactic four-mile manhunt through the woods and swamp was shot on a 120-by-200-foot soundstage, with the crew continuously repositioning trees and shrubs to create the illusion of distance covered. Working with Borzage, art director Lionel Banks skillfully designed this sequence, reducing a $120,000 location shoot to just $28,000. Lillian Gish was slotted to play Danny's grandmother in the revelatory penultimate scene, but when her Broadway play *Crime and Punishment* was extended, Ethel Barrymore replaced her—earning a hefty $25,000 for two days' work.

The film ends, as the book does, on a note of moral regeneration and spiritual transcendence as Danny surrenders and is reunited with Gilly. But its dark, somber tone makes the film feel more like a surreal nightmare. *Moonrise* received mixed reviews and tanked at the box office. Its reputation was rehabilitated later, distinguished by its being the sole noir on Borzage's considerable résumé.

The director seldom spoke about the film, regarding it as an experiment: "A moving picture in sound as opposed to a talking film." He became increasingly disillusioned with the studio system and abandoned moviemaking for ten years. He made only two more pictures before his death in 1962.

Theodore Strauss did not fare much better. He never wrote another book, and his once highly acclaimed novel—a Hollywood "hot property"—was forgotten as quickly as the film. When it was reissued in paperback by Bantam Books in 1951, *Moonrise* was retitled *Dark Hunger*. ∎

BOOK VS. FILM
Nora Fiore

Hidden among the slippery boulders of a mean river, the Kid waits for the right moment. Then he snags a large, unpleasant fish—the kind that goes around on two legs and carries a .45. Slats, the fish in question, does not stand a chance:

He saw it coming. He saw the bright bit of metal before it hit him. He saw wet line arching away. But he was not quick enough. The spinner's hooks bit through his shirt into his chest and he felt the barbs sink in as the line went taut. He pitched forward and saw the river coming up to meet him.

With a flick of his casting rod, the Kid not only put the hook into Slats, but also RKO producer Warren Duff.

"That was one of the things that sold the book to pictures, the gimmick of the kid using a casting rod to pull the guy off the cliff," author Daniel Mainwaring remembered. "Duff fell in love with that and bought the book." The book being *Build My Gallows High* (1946), written under Mainwaring's pen name, Geoffrey Homes. Duff was less enchanted with Mainwaring's attempt at adapting his own work. He hired other hands: novelist James M. Cain, Frank Fenton. Layers of revisions may have muddied the plot, but the writers' pooled wits amounted to a peerless flow of quotable dialogue.

Out of the Past (1947) hews to the general storyline of *Gallows*. Private eye Jeff Markham once set out to find a racketeer's mistress, but ran away with her instead. Now Jeff, alias Bailey (but mostly called "Red" in the book), makes his living with a small-town gas station and dreams of settling down with local girl Ann. Until an outsider turns up and pulls Red back into the dangerous world of his former associates. Red's mission with lawyer Leonard Eels takes him to New York, rather than San Francisco, in the book. However, the affidavit frame-up plays out similarly, except that the novel's murder of Meta Carson adds another corpse to the body count. Bailey flees back to the country, where he strives to stay ahead of the cops and turn the tables on his enemies.

For the film's laconic lead, Mainwaring suggested Humphrey Bogart, but the role cemented Robert Mitchum's stardom instead. Jeff Bailey thus links two of noir's greatest leading men. While many of Bailey's best wisecracks were scripted for the film, the novel's Red has a non-

Daniel Mainwaring with Humphrey Bogart, the author's first choice to play Bailey in the film adaptation.

A noir match for the ages: Robert Mitchum as the world-weary ex–private eye and Jane Greer as the ruthless femme fatale.

chalant sense of humor suited to both Bogart's and Mitchum's personas. In one memorable maneuver, lost in the translation to film, Red fills a suitcase with Gideon Bibles instead of sought-after tax papers. When his foes steal the decoy, Red quips, "He's welcome to it. It may bring him salvation."

For starlet Jane Greer, the film's diabolical Kathie Moffat was "a part made in heaven." *Out of the Past* reshapes the audience's perception of the femme fatale by revealing her ruthlessness earlier in the plot. The novel's siren bears the cumbersome moniker Mumsie McGonigle, more appropriate for a bridge-playing matron than a larcenous moll. "I'll never be any good," Mumsie admits to Red. "Such a black soul, darling." Thief and liar though she is, Mumsie does not pull the trigger to silence Jeff's former partner, Fisher. Instead, he dies while struggling with Jeff for the gun. As Jeff digs a grave, Mumsie disappears into the night. Such an anticlimactic breakup pales in comparison to the film's cabin fight scene. In one of the writers' most brilliant alterations, Kathie watches the men duke it out in the flickering firelight, then coolly dispatches Fisher (Steve Brodie). With Mitchum's look of understated shock, Bailey's passion curdles into disillusion.

The film also expands the temptress's role. Although Mumsie's liaison with Red incites the novel's events, she is more remembered and referred to than present. In the novel's final pages, Red recognizes Mumsie as "the spinner of the web" that finally catches him, but she works in elusive ways. While Red and Whit haggle over which fall guy or gal to hand over to the cops—a scene reminiscent of *The Maltese Falcon*—Mumsie is nowhere to be seen. In *Out of the Past*, Kathie listens as the men determine her fate, the audience seeing the wheels turn as her demeanor shifts from terror to resolve. Whereas Mumsie mostly lurks in the background, Kathie actively wheedles, supervises, schemes, and sometimes calls the shots.

The screenplay and Jacques Tourneur's direction refocus the story on Jeff and Kathie's poisonous mutual desire. The embers of Red's romantic feelings for Mumsie have long since burnt out in Mainwaring's novel. As Red remarks, "Love's easy to kill." But the electricity between Jeff and Kathie in *Out of the Past* continues to spark. The script invents later scenes between the duo, giving Kathie time to dig her claws into Jeff once again. Nicholas Musuraca's cinematography and the actors' chemistry keep the viewer enthralled by the perverse romance. Their starkly sensual backlit kiss in the San Francisco apartment captures the fire-and-ice essence of noir's *amour fou*.

The film's Whit Sterling fuses the novel's two villains into one. In both the book and the film, the gambler-racketeer hires Bailey to find his trigger-happy mistress. But the sinister figure who yanks Red out of his unassuming idyll is former police chief Guy Parker, summoning the ex-shamus and sending him on a fall guy's errand to the big city. In the end, Red discovers that a vengeful Whit is orchestrating the plot. *Out of the Past* sacrifices the predictable twist of Whit's involvement in favor of suspense. The audience understands that Bailey is walking into a trap from the moment Kirk Douglas's Whit smugly resurfaces. The elimination of Parker makes for a more elegant plotline. Parker's flagrant corruption might have also resulted in additional friction with the Production Code Administration, which found more than enough to reproach in the film's sexual dynamics.

The emotional core of *Out of the Past* is its flashback, a device borrowed from the novel. After encountering his old flame at Parker's mansion, Red cannot sleep: "He thought about Mumsie and wondered if she had changed much inside. A strange dame Mumsie. His mind went back ten years . . ." The film raises the dramatic stakes by setting up the flashback as a painful confession to a loved one. Mitchum's Bailey is not merely remembering, but *telling* the story to Ann. As they drive toward Whit's lair in the night, Jeff warns her, "Some of it's gonna hurt you." Every unpleasant turn of his story deals a double blow: to Jeff in the past and to Ann in the present.

On the whole, Mainwaring approved of the film, except "that mother in Bridgeport." The film's judgmental Mrs. Miller (Adda Gleason) does grate on the viewer's nerves, but Ann's mother in the novel is no paragon of understanding either. At least she has the distinction of "finding solace in the bloodthirsty antics of her favorite comic characters." Perhaps Mainwaring found the mother more obnoxious without the counterbalance that Ann's sympathetic father provides in the novel.

While the film flattens some characters, it puts a witty spin on others, particularly Joe Stefanos. As

"We deserve each other." *Out of the Past* embellished the deadly attraction between Bailey and Whit's moll.

Greer and Mitchum relax between takes of *Out of the Past*. Greer remembered her costar as "a great friend."

with Whit, *Out of the Past*'s Stefanos reduces two villains into one. The novel's main henchmen, Stefanos and Slats, are typical coldblooded specimens. A more entertaining creation, Paul Valentine's shady, ineffectual right-hand man combines comic relief and danger. When odd-men-out Fisher and Stefanos exchange fireside glances, the beat of humiliated recognition lands like a silent punchline. The film's Stefanos winces at the memory of a man too scared to pray—a man he killed all the same.

The plotlines of *Out of the Past* and *Build My Gallows High* diverge toward the end. In a desperate bid for freedom, Jeff plans to run to Mexico, where Ann will join him. The novel concludes with Red sneaking into Parker's mansion to retrieve Mumsie's cache of money. Mumsie stops those dreams with a bullet. Red barely makes it out the door. Such a grim, matter-of-fact finale would scarcely suit the twisted love story that *Out of the Past* had become.

In a scene unique to the film, Kathie tells Jeff that he is going away with her. Although the novel observes that "you couldn't make deals with a dead man," the film puts those words in Kathie's mouth almost verbatim. During their love-hate duet on the balcony, Bailey references the film's original title, changed at the urging of Gallup's Audience Research Institute. Faced with Kathie's threats, Jeff replies, "Build my gallows high, baby." A line that would sink most actors becomes a dare, a come-on, a rebuke, and a wry capitulation all at once in Mitchum's delivery.

Out of the Past's explosive finale parallels the ending of another torrid RKO noir: *Born to Kill*, filmed earlier in 1946. After losing her meal ticket, a furious Helen Brent (Claire Trevor) betrays her homicidal soulmate, Sam Wilde (Lawrence Tierney). Infuriated by her betrayal, Sam shoots her, then crumples in a hail of police bullets. The ending of *Out of the Past* follows a similar pattern, with different psychological implications. Jeff's stealthy call to the police prompts a roadblock showdown. As Kathie's mask of elegant poise slips into a snarl of guttersnipe fury, she shoots the "double-crossing rat" before the machine gun fire takes her down too. Jeff chooses to die with Kathie rather than live with her—a nuance not lost on Joseph Breen. The censor objected to Bailey's suicidal finish, but allowed it as a punishment for the antihero's sins.

Despite the many narrative changes between the novel and its adaptation, they share a sense of exultation in nature. Driving to confront Whit, Red falls into a reverie, like Thoreau in the key of hardboiled private eye: "As always, when he looked down on the big lake, he felt his spirits lift. You didn't amount to anything and what happened to you didn't matter." Tourneur harnesses the bracing beauty of the High Sierras and other California locations to heighten the tragedy of Jeff's shattered happiness. The distant peaks, sparkling waters, and sunshine contrast with shadowy, oppressive urban spaces. *Out of the Past*'s autumnal landscapes imbue the film with a mysterious quality of wonder and a yearning poetry in the spirit of Mainwaring's descriptions. The novel even closes on a note of communion with nature. Bleeding out from Mumsie's bullet, Red enjoys the view one last time before crashing to earth: "He'd miss those hills, he thought. He'd miss those clouds. *Look up once more. Up. Up.* He didn't hear the gun when Guy shot him because he was dead."

Instead of ending with Jeff's demise, *Out of the Past* leaves the viewer haunted by one of noir's most poignant parting shots. The Kid lies with a nod, confirming to Ann that Bailey wanted to go away with Kathie. After releasing the girl from her devotion to a dead man, the Kid salutes Jeff's name on the gas station sign. Then he turns and walks away from the camera. He alone knows the truth about Bailey. The choice to end the film on the Kid's melancholy gesture may reflect an earlier concept of the script with a flashback narrated by the Kid. Although the novel explores the Kid's thoughts, Dickie Moore's performance conveys his interiority without a mawkish voice-over. The final shot, with its barren tree and faraway mountains, aches with loss and lonely secrets. The eloquence of Tourneur's images equals and surpasses the film's source material. As the Kid knows well, life's most profound emotions need no words to be expressed. ■

For a select bibliography, please visit bit.ly/BMGH-book-to-film.

NOIR WAS BORN AT THE CORNER OF ...

HOLLYWOOD BLVD. 6300W

CRIME ST. 1800N

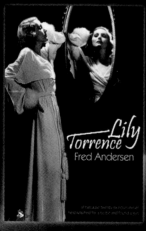

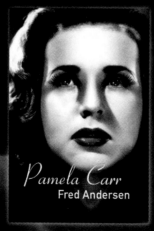

Classic Hollywood Murder Mysteries by Fred Andersen
fxandersen.com

CONTRIBUTORS

Ray Banks is the author of eleven novels, including the Cal Innes Quartet and, most recently, *Trouble's Braids* (2017). He lives in Fife, Scotland.

Brent Calderwood is an arts and culture writer, editor, and author. His essays and profiles appear in *Rolling Stone*, *Cineaste*, *Out*, and *NOIR CITY Magazine*. He has received awards, fellowships, and grants from the Lambda Literary Foundation, the San Francisco Public Library, Poets & Writers, and elsewhere. His book of poems, *The God of Longing*, was an American Library Association selection for 2014. His website is brentcalderwood.com.

Danilo Castro is the managing editor of *NOIR CITY Magazine*. He has contributed to several other publications including PopMatters and *Little White Lies*.

Chris D. (aka Chris Desjardins) is the singer/songwriter of the bands The Flesh Eaters and Divine Horsemen. He was a film programmer at The American Cinematheque in Hollywood from 1999 – 2009 and taught film history/film genre courses at The Academy of Art University in San Francisco from 2009 – 2013. He is also the author of five novels, one short story collection and the 800-page, non-fiction *Gun and Sword: An Encyclopedia of Japanese Gangster Films 1955–1980*. He also wrote and directed the neo-noir/horror saga, *I Pass for Human*, released on DVD in 2006.

Nora Fiore has contributed to Flicker Alley, Kino Lorber, Indicator, Arrow Academy, and Olive Films Blu-ray releases. She blogs and posts on social media as The Nitrate Diva.

Lynsey Ford is an arts and culture writer from Wimbledon, London. Her film essays and profiles have been published by The British Film Institute, *Little White Lies*, *Scream Horror*, *The Guardian*, The Culture Trip, *Variety*, *Cineaste*, and *NOIR CITY Magazine* (amongst others). She is a Fellow of The Royal Society of Arts and is an Associate Fellow from The Royal Historical Society. Her website is lynseyford.space.

Jake Hinkson is the author of several novels, including the recent *Find Him*, as well as the essay collection *The Blind Alley: Exploring Film Noir's Forgotten Corners*. His fiction has been translated into French, German, and Italian. In 2018, his novel *No Tomorrow* was awarded the *Grand Prix des Littératures Policière*, France's most prestigious award for crime and detective fiction.

Vince Keenan is the former Editor-in-Chief of *NOIR CITY Magazine* (2020 - 2022). With his wife Rosemarie Keenan, he writes the Lillian Frost and Edith Head mysteries (*Design for Dying*, *Dangerous to Know*, *The Sharpest Needle*, *Idle Gossip*) under the pen name Renee Patrick. He is also the author of *Down the Hatch: One Man's One Year Odyssey Through Classic Cocktail Recipes and Lore*.

Sharon Knolle is an LA-based writer whose bylines include *Variety*, *USA Today*, Moviefone, and IMDb. She won two 2022 Southern California Journalism Awards for her writing as a reporter at TheWrap.

Steve Kronenberg is the managing editor of *NOIR CITY Magazine*. He has served as co-publisher and contributor to the classic horror magazine *Monsters from the Vault* and is co-author of *The Creature Chronicles: Exploring the Black Lagoon Trilogy* and *Universal Terrors 1951-1955*, both published by McFarland and Company. Steve is a contributing writer to publications *Ringside Seat*, *Classic Images*, and *Films of the Golden Age*.

Brian Light, NOIR CITY: Hollywood showrunner, has contributed program notes for various Los Angeles County Museum of Art film series such as *The Naked City: New York Noir and Neorealism*, *2012: A Kubrick Odyssey*, and *Animating the Subconscious*. He has also published a series of articles on the global rockabilly scene for Billboard. Most recently, Brian curated "Global Hollywood," an exhibition of his film noir poster collection funded by the Hollywood Foreign Press Association, at California State University, Northridge.

Sam Moore is a freelance culture writer in the UK. His essays and interviews have been featured in *The Guardian*, *Financial Times*, *GQ*, *Interview Magazine*, *Little White Lies*, *Daily Telegraph*, NME, and *Esquire* among others.

Farran Smith Nehme has written about film and film history for The Criterion Collection, *Sight and Sound*, *Film Comment*, *The Village Voice*, the *New York Post*, *Barron's*, *The Wall Street Journal*, and *The New York Times*, as well as for her blog, Self-Styled Siren, which can be found on Substack. Her novel, *Missing Reels*, was published in 2014.

Bob Sassone is a columnist for *The Saturday Evening Post* and the author of the essay collection *Book, with Words and Pages*. He lives in Massachusetts where he's working on a novel.

Imogen Sara Smith, Editor-in-Chief of *NOIR CITY Magazine* since 2023, is the author of *In Lonely Places: Film Noir Beyond the City*. Based in New York City, she has written for *Film Comment*, *Sight and Sound*, *Reverse Shot*, The Criterion Collection, and many other journals, and is a frequent commentator on The Criterion Channel and on Blu-ray discs. Imogen teaches film history at NYU and Maine Media Workshops. She is currently working on a biography of Lauren Bacall for Oxford University Press.

Jim Thomsen is a writer, editor, former newspaperman. and non-certified (but certifiable) Seventiesologist. His fiction and nonfiction have been published in *Shotgun Honey*, *Mystery Tribune*, *Switchblade*, *Pulp Modern*, and *The Rap Sheet*. He makes his home in Kingston, Washington.

Rachel Walther is the film columnist for *Hamam* magazine. Based in Oakland, California, she has worked with Music Box Films, Facets Multimedia, and Amoeba Records. Her personal site, Sleeping All Day, features essays on modern crime films and late twentieth-century culture.

John Wranovics is the author of *Chaplin and Agee*. John's writing on film and social history has appeared in *The New York Times*, *Positif*, *Capricci 2011*, *Film Watch*, and various academic anthologies and conferences.

"Fate...It's All in the Cards"   *lithograph from stone 11" x 14" 2019*

To purchase original
ANN CHERNOW
lithographs and etchings

Call: Connecticut Fine Arts at
(203)-227-1302

Email: annctfinearts@gmail.com